You Can Get
What You Want
if
You Find It
Within Yourself

◆

ROBERT A. RUSSELL

Martino Fine Books
Eastford, CT
2024

Martino Fine Books
P.O. Box 913,
Eastford, CT 06242 USA

ISBN   978-1-68422-859-1

Copyright 2024

Martino Fine Books

Cover Design Tiziana Matarazzo

Printed in the United States of America On 100% Acid-Free Paper

You Can Get What You Want

if

You Find It Within Yourself

◆

ROBERT A. RUSSELL

EPIPHANY EPISCOPAL CHURCH
The Shrine of the Healing Presence
100 Colorado Boulevard
Denver 7, Colorado

NOTE TO THE STUDENT

This book is one of a series of four consecutive metaphysical studies on the Parable of the Prodigal Son and the Elder Brother. The books are listed in the order that they should be read.

1. IF YOU FIND IT WITHIN YOURSELF

2. IF YOU RETURN HOME

3. IF YOU PUT THIS FIRST

4. IF YOU TALK YOURSELF INTO IT

INDEX

Page

Creative Power Chart... 6
Explanation of Creative Power 7
Introduction 9
God Must Work Through Our Intelligence 11
Grief 16
Two Selves 17
Center of Being 20
The Empty House 30
I Came Not to Destroy, But to Fulfill 36
Selflessness 39
Meeting Your Problems Where You Are................. 51
The Inner Realm Is the Realm of Cause 54
A Metaphysical Rosary 67
Healing 73
Resolve Everything Into Thoughts 75
What Must I Do to Be Saved?............................ 79
Change the Subjective Causes............................. 82
True Prayer 86
Seek the Aboveness of Life 90
Missing the Mark 99
Formula for Restoration of the "I" 108
Harnessing the Power 111
Runaways 117
The Things that Need Altering 121
Looking Back 126
Decide 131
Blessed Is the Man Who Keeps Growing 134
Faith in Your Goal...136
One Mind 140
Turn to the Chart 145
Belief in Separation 148
Lovingly in the Hands of the Father 150
God Does Not Know Evil 156
Equanimity 161
The Way to Conquer Difficulties 163
Specializing the Power 166
God Is Not an Almshouse Keeper 169
Breaking the Power of Circumstance 171

LIFE AS IT IS, AND AS PLANNED BY GOD..

**HEALTH, SUCCESS, JOY, HAPPINESS, STRENGTH, DOMINION
WEALTH, FAITH, CONFIDENCE, CERTAINTY, PEACE, POWER
PLENTY, POISE, COURAGE, LOVE, HARMONY, FREEDOM**

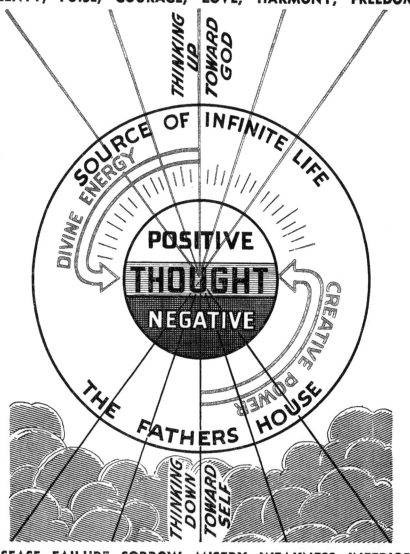

**DISEASE, FAILURE, SORROW, MISERY, WEAKNESS, INFERIOR
ITY, POVERTY, UNHAPPINESS, WORRY, FEAR, DOUBT, LOSS
TROUBLE, LIMITATIONS, DISCORD, PROBLEMS, BONDAGE**

LIFE AS WE MAKE IT BY OUR NEGATIVE THINKING

EXPLANATION OF DIAGRAM

If you will study the diagram on the opposite page, you will see that the power flowing from God through man is neither good nor bad as the human mind usually understands it. It is simply Divine Energy—Creative Power. The energy that is turned into failure, sickness and discord and other negative expressions in no way differs from the energy that manifests in success, health, peace and other forms of good. The difference is not in the energy, or Creative Power, but in the thought that turns it either into constructive or destructive channels.

How important it is, then, that we should keep our thought centered in the constructive and affirmative side of Good and guarded against the destructive side of evil, so that only the good can manifest in our lives—the riches of life instead of its limitations.

NOTE TO THE STUDENT

The Author asks that before beginning the study of this book you read thoughtfully the Parable of The Prodigal Son as found in the fifteenth chapter of St. Luke's Gospel.

INTRODUCTION

Success in spiritual work as in anything else is a matter of understanding, consciousness, method and technique. Our world is a world of cause and effect. As we sow so shall we reap, and to reap profitably we must sow intelligently. Emerson said, "Every soul is not only the inlet but may become the outlet of all there is in God."

If the chemist puts two chemicals together, he gets a certain definite reaction. If the artist puts two colors together, he gets another color. If the Truth student puts his mind together with God's Mind (keeps an open communication between the two), he gets what he wants. He gets it because he is *en rapport* with God, or open to receive.

Just as God's thoughts and words are creative, so our thoughts and words are creative. They are creative because we are made in God's Image and share His Mind. God is Responsive Intelligence. He is good, coming at our call in our greatest or slightest need— Good manifested for us instantly, if the acknowledgment be there and the realization be strong enough. Thus, when we ask God for anything we are sure of an affirmative answer if we have truly put into our prayer what we hope to take out of it.

The secret of getting what is wanted from Life is to find it within ourselves as an idea (let it form in us a consciousness of itself), and then to let it flow through us into the visible. The continued acknowledgment and realization of a thought as true, plus sustained attention to it, creates a mental equivalent, or affinity, for that thing. The mental equivalent held firmly in the conscious mind is then passed on to the subconscious mind, where it is acted upon by Divine Substance and produces a harvest exactly like itself.

Thus, what we accept as true in the within becomes true in the without. "Out of the heart (subconscious mind) are the issues of life." "As a man thinketh in his heart (subconscious mind), so is he." Prayer is not a game of chance, as when one puts a nickel into a slot machine and gets two nickels or hits the jack pot. Prayer is providing a mental equivalent, or belief, through which God's attributes can be expressed.

God is not divided into a lot of separate attributes to be taken as one would take medicines for specific ailments, but is a perfect whole, indivisible and inseparable. His attributes cannot be parceled out for specific needs as one would use alkalies as an antidote for acids, but each one must express everything that God is. Life, Love, Truth, Substance, Wisdom and Power are only different names for God, and each one pressed through the mind expresses the others proportionately. If we involve love and truth in the mind, then health and prosperity will evolve with them. God cannot express part of his attributes through us: He must express all or none.

Just as all the water in the ocean tries to get through a hole in the ship, so all the attributes of God press against the mind that is in harmony with Him. If we express wisdom, then we shall also express understanding. If we express wealth, then we shall also express well-being. If we express life, then we shall also express strength.

GOD MUST WORK THROUGH OUR INTELLIGENCE

God will do anything for us that He can do through us, but He cannot do anything from the outside. He must work through our intelligence. If we want Him to think for us, speak for us, decide for us, act for us and pray for us, then we must give Him our minds and thoughts. Jesus said, "Seek ye first the Kingdom of God, and His righteousness; and all these things shall be added unto you." This means that if you look inside for everything then you shall find everything you are looking for. But if you look to the outside for your help then you shall find only frustration and disappointment.

Just as the moving picture projector continually expresses upon the screen what is on the film, so the consciousness continually expresses what is in the mind. To change the expression on the screen we must change the film, and to change the expression in the world we must change the image in the mind. "Man looketh on the outward appearance, but God looketh on the heart." It is easy to demonstrate things when we work from the inside out and impossible when we work from the outside in.

"My God shall supply all your needs according to His riches in Christ Jesus in glory." Now read this passage again and see if you can discover the key by which this promised supply is released. Note the unusual arrangement of our Lord's Name as contrasted with other references to Him in the New Testament. It does not say according to His riches in Jesus Christ, but "According to His riches in CHRIST Jesus." Why do you suppose St. Paul put the name "Christ" before "Jesus" in this instance? He did it to show us that God's supply comes from the inside instead of from the outside. It was always "Christ in you the hope of glory;" "Let Christ be formed in you;" "Let this Mind be in you which was also in CHRIST Jesus," etc., etc.

When Jesus said that "The Kingdom of God is within you," He meant that everything Good is already within you. Then how do you release this Good into expression? By your constant acknowledgment and realization of it. As you impress the truth of a thought upon your subconscious mind it expresses back to you from the Universe as an object, or favorable condition in your affairs. To know God you must express Him. That is, you must press out from the Center of your Being all those things which are like the Center. To realize God in all your affairs, you must see God in everything and everybody.

"In love is love reflected." In God is Good reflected. If you give love to a dog, he will give his friendship to you. If you deal truthfully with others, they will deal truthfully with you. If you give out helpfulness, helpfulness will come back to you. Why? Because God's attributes are in everybody, and as you call them out of yourself you call them out of others also. That is the way the Universe is made and that is the way the Law works. "Do unto others as you would have them do unto you."

When your mind is harmonized with God's Mind, there is always a reciprocal action between your thoughts and God's thoughts. What you give out or send out always comes back to you, whether it be for good or ill. The Law is impersonal and the harvest will always be according to the sowing. It makes no difference how good and upright you may be on the surface, if you are harboring evil thoughts within then you will reap a harvest of evil in the outer world.

Your friends may say, "He was such a good man, I don't see why this evil had to happen to him." It happened to him because he had an unseen affinity for it, his outer behavior and his inner behavior were not in accord. It makes no difference how good a person may be on the surface, if he has inward fears of accidents, disease and failure, then he will attract those things and have them in his experience; yes, even though he prays to be delivered from them.

That is why Jesus told us to seek His Kingdom first. What did He mean? He meant that we were to make His Kingdom real to our own minds. How do we do that? By constant acknowledgment and realization of it. If you would receive something from God, then you must first be that thing. You must have it in consciousness as a mental equivalent, and then you must give (express) it out. Does that sound like a paradox? Then, it means simply that all receiving begins with giving. "Give, and it shall be given unto you."

To seek God's Kingdom, to which all material things are added, means to realize the Omnipresence of God and to make Him omnipresent in everything you think, say, give and do. It means to express His attributes in everything, everywhere, at all times. Heaven is actually everywhere, and when you realize and accept this fact Heaven will be in all places for you.

GRIEF

The reason fleshly-minded people grieve so much when a loved one leaves this plane is because they think of life, or Heaven, as being in some other time or place. When the heart is broken or heavy with grief, the lodge and the fraternal order will not give it peace. Peace comes only from the consciousness of the Omnipresence of God and because of the everywhereness of His Spirit. We sing of the beautiful isle of somewhere—that isle is NOW, HERE.

The people who suffer most in physical separation are those who are most material in their thought. They are those who think farthest out away from the Spiritual Center, and the farther away they are from that Center the more they suffer. Life to them is only what they see physically and when they no longer can see with the material vision they are lost in grief. Having separated the personality (body) from the individuality (Spirit), they have nothing to cling to. They see the shadow instead of the Light which casts it. They love the shadow more than the Light, and when the shadow disappears their light goes out. Then they are bewildered, defeated.

When God sought to temper the wrath of the Elder Brother upon the Prodigal's return home, He said: "Son, thou art ever with me, and all that I have is thine." As God's son you are His heir. You are potentially and have potentially everything that God is or has. As you find Him—Good, in things close to you, then you shall begin to see Him in the things that are all about you.

Dwelling on God's Omnipresence is like starting a fire in dry grass on a windy day. The fire will grow and spread with such tremendous speed and power that it will consume quickly every appearance unlike itself. God is omnipresent but you must become aware of it. If you would have Him expressing Himself through you, then you must express His attributes through your own consciousness.

TWO SELVES

In the Being of Jesus there were two distinct selves. There was the human, personal self, Jesus the son of man; and there was the Divine, Spiritual, Real Self that was the Christ or Son of God. So, as St. Paul said, there are two selves in every man—"There is a natural body, and there is a spiritual body." Whether our experiences are good or bad depends upon which self is in the ascendancy.

The natural body is the fleshly, mortal part of us, which is always feeling its limitations, separations, defeats, disappointments and illnesses; always judging according to appearances and always seeing evil. And there is within this body, but not of it, the "Spiritual Body," made in the image and likeness of God, "of one substance with the Father," eternal in the heavens, continually nourished and renewed from Its Source and instant conqueror of error and all the destructive forces in our lives.

"For ye are the temple of the living God: as God hath said, I will dwell in them, and walk in them." The Temple of the Living God is the Spiritual body, or temple, of perfection. It is that Higher part of our being, which when recognized, realized and lived in will arrest all deterioration, destruction and stagnation in the lower, or "natural body." Bringing yourself under the law of God, the human laws of weakness, sickness and decay will no more be operative for you. As the Bible says, you will be above them and no more subject to them.

Spinoza said, "Substance is plastic and

Spirit is compelling." The outer body is only a vehicle. It is helpless and powerless unless acted upon or animated by some superior force. "The flesh profiteth nothing"—that is, it does not produce anything. It must act in conjunction with something else. That is what Job meant when he said, "Yet in my flesh shall I see God." When we return to the Father's House (live again at the Center) and radiate from that Center that which the Center is (perfection and wholeness), then we shall see Spirit materialized in our flesh.

The Parable of the Prodigal Son is, in reality, the story of every man who leaves the Center of his being to live on its circumference. It is the story of what happens to every one who shifts the center of his spiritual gravity from soul to sense. Do you need confirmation of this fact? Then look at your own life from the perimeter (outer boundary of the body) and you will see that there is very little there that looks like God. That is why the outer man must be rejoined to the Christ. The lion and the lamb shall lie down together. The prodigal must return home. The circumference and Center must become one. Mastery begins in surrender.

Jesus understood this perfectly and that is why He always identified Himself with the Christ and why He never gave power to the suggestions coming to Him from the outer world. "The prince of this world cometh," He said, "and findeth nothing in me." That is the reason why He kept His thoughts centered in the Christ, or God-Side, of His Being. "Of mine own (personal) self," He said, "I can do nothing. The Father within, He doeth the works." It was always the Inner Man—the Father Within, the Power within, the Heaven within, the substance within, the supply within, and His invitations were always to the Central, or Christ, part of His being.

THE CENTER OF BEING

It was always: Come to the Center. Trust the Center. Rely on the Center. Hold fast to the Center. Abide in the Center. Live in the Center. Think in the Center. Act from the Center. Work from the Center. Draw from the Center. Give from the Center. Radiate from the Center. Indeed, the whole burden of His ministry was to call men back from the circumference to the Center and to show them how to radiate from that Center the abundant life of Spirit and the blessings of Heaven.

But let us go back again to Emerson's statement. "Every soul is not only the inlet but may become the outlet of all there is in God." All that any one of us may become on this earth plane is determined by what we let flow through our consciousness. "A jug may contain pure platinum as easily as it may contain wine." A man may receive and express the stream of life flowing out from the heart of God as easily as he can allow the appearance of the world to flow through him. It is all a matter of the Source from which he draws his impressions. He draws into his nature that which holds his attention and that which he relies upon.

"How then shall we destroy these old impressions which have kept us in such misery?" By cultivating new ones. Faith in God grows through practice and false beliefs die through neglect. When Jesus said, "Judge not according to the appearances, but judge righteous judgment," He meant that we were to discipline ourselves out of our old habits and beliefs by refusing to express and exercise them, and that we were to give ourselves to the faithful application of Truth and the formation of new habits.

The trouble with most people is that they believe in a power over them instead of a power within them. Listen to Zephaniah, 3:17: "The Lord thy God in the midst of thee is mighty; He will save; He will rejoice over thee with joy; He will rest in His love, He will joy over thee with singing." All you have to do is to be in the Center (active in the right direction) and God will do the rest. "The Lord thy God in the midst of thee is mighty." No circumstance or combination of circumstances; nor trouble or combination of troubles; no problem or combination of problems; no disease however terrible can withstand the Power of God. "Fear not ye, neither be dismayed by reason of this great multitude; for the battle is not yours, but God's."

You are not to be driven and tossed by your own thought of things. It was your own thought (acting from the circumference) that got you into the trouble in the first place. "The words I speak are not mine," said Jesus, "but the Father's in me." None of us has very much power by ourselves, but, when we unite our power with God's Power, then we have unlimited power. We are then working "under grace," so to speak, and "can do all things through Christ which strengtheneth us."

We all marvel at the amazing power of Jesus but we forget many times that this same power is in us. The secret of Jesus' great spiritual strength was not in some special gift or divine favor from on high, but in His ability to act from the Center of His Being, instead of from its circumference. He acted not from the outer edge of His personality, but from the Central, Living part of His Being, which was God. Speaking from the consciousness of Christ, His words were confirmed by the world. He could control everything of the world because He was not controlled by anything in the world.

Fear not, then, the great calamity that has come upon you, the person who threatens you, the disease that weakens you, the limitations that impoverish you, the failure that frightens you. Fear only the loss of the consciousness of God's Presence, and then reach through that fear into unity with Him. Fear only the temptation to believe in evil, and then do something about it.

As Emerson said, "Do the thing and you shall find that you have the power." Get a firmer connection with the Christ Within. Live at the Center and hold fast to the Truth. Go through every appearance of evil to the Spirit back of it. If God is everywhere, then He is in the very things that seem painful and disagreeable to you. Keep your thoughts on Christ and away from the circumference. "Judge not according to the appearances;" that is, according to the seeming, "but judge righteous judgment," according to the inward Reality, or Truth.

In other words, forget what is happening on the surface and think of God, and not evil, as being there. No matter how destructive and powerful the evil may seem, we must remember that in Spirit all is good. Back of all Creation is God and, to bring forth the good, we must see the Good in the Spirit back of it. We cannot change evil into good by working with effects. We must go behind the realm of effects to the realm of causes, where all is good. Our thoughts are creative in the right direction when they are centered in perfect God-Substance, which is everywhere equally present. We change effects by changing causes.

"But as many as received Him to them gave He power." If our thought is not centered in God (if we have not received Him), then we are in the personal consciousness and we are weak. We are weak because we have cut ourselves off from the Parent Stem. We have not cultivated the Christ. We are, as it were, living in our own strength and having nothing to hold us up. "God is a very present help in trouble," as the Psalmist said, but His help is given only to those who are present, or centered in Him.

If our unity with God is intermittent and weak, like an electric light bulb screwed loosely into the socket, then we shall continue to fluctuate between light and darkness, between good and evil. It wouldn't make any difference, you see, how good the lamp, nor how much power the wires may carry, if the connection be intermittent the light too will be intermittent. It will sputter on and off uncertainly. So it is in our spiritual work. To keep the Power of God in expression, we must be constant and unwavering in our realization of His Good.

Jesus said, "My Father worketh hitherto, and I work." The Father's work is to supply our needs and our work is to supply the connection and the measures in which to receive them. Our Good depends not upon God alone but upon our receptivity to His Bounties. To get good results from prayer, we must be good transmitters of Divine Power. We must keep our thought clear of all obstructions. That is why Jesus said, "Leave all and follow me."

Take your attention away from everything that may be troubling you and place it upon God. Drop everything also from your thought and cultivate the consciousness of that Mind from which you came. Recapture the glory which you had with God before the world was; that is, before you adulterated your consciousness with so many false beliefs.

Are you troubled about your body? Then give it to God and let Him renew it. Jesus referred to man's body as a temple, and St. Paul said, "Be ye transformed by the renewing of your mind." Did you ever see this renewing process at work in yourself, so evident that your friends noticed it and asked what you were doing?

The same thing has happened to the dilapidated house that you set about to make over. The porch sags; the doors are off their hinges; windows are dirty and broken; the plaster is cracked; the stairs are falling apart; the roof leaks; the paint is drab and cracked; the chimney has fallen in; the plumbing is rusty and clogged, the chandeliers have broken loose from their moorings.

You buy the place and determine to renew it. Plumbers come to fix the plumbing; plasterers and carpenters look after the woodwork and the plaster; glaziers replace the windows; painters decorate and restore the walls; bricklayers build a new chimney; interior decorators hang drapes and refurnish the rooms; electricians repair the wiring. Finally the house is made over, renovated, redecorated, refurnished, renewed, and this is what St. Paul meant by being transformed.

Our subconscious minds are just like this old house—filled with antiquated fears, worries, doubts, limitations, inhibitions, ghosts, and negative beliefs. We have lost sight of the indwelling, everactive and everrenewing Christ at the Center, and we are in every way miserable, limited and inferior. Disintegration has set in and we are daily going to rack and ruin. Instead of being young, prosperous, well and strong, we are old, poor, sick and weak.

Then how will you set about to renew the house called "you"? There is but one way, as St. Paul said, "Put off the old man and put on the new man, which is Christ." This means to cleanse your consciousness of all error; to drop out of it every thought and belief that keeps you in bondage, that makes you susceptible to dissolution and decay.

Pull down the unsightly old beliefs that are destroying your happiness and peace of mind. Demolish the fears that are holding you in bondage. Wash the windows that are obscuring the Truth. Remove the worries that are causing your structure to settle. Rehang the door that is barring your good. Rebuild the stairs of prayer that have fallen down. Relight the fire of unity on the hearth. "Let this Mind be in you which was also in Christ Jesus." Let Him heal the gaps in your consciousness. Let Him repair and renew your mind. Let Him have your intelligence, your thoughts and your body.

"Behold, I make all things new." Surrender lifts the structure into place; Confidence hangs the door; Faith repairs the broken stairs; Singleness of Vision cleans the windows; Love restores the walls; Unity purifies the whole house. The body and mind are renewed. "Old things are passed away: behold, all things are become new." Troubles are dissolved; difficulties are removed; desires are purified; motives are chastened; activities are transformed; thoughts are unified; fear gives way to faith; sorrow gives way to joy; sickness gives way to health; discord gives way to peace; despair gives way to hope; commonplace things become lustrous; disagreeable things become pleasurable. The glory of the Lord fills the temple and it is made new.

And the new man is just the old man with new thoughts and new combinations. Just as one organist will bring out from the organ harsh, discordant and wild strains that jar on the nerves and cause a feeling of irritation and discomfort, so another will send forth from the same instrument melodies that soothe, uplift and quiet the nerves. But there is still another Organist Who surpasses them all. He is the originator, designer and maker of the organ and has planned all its beauties and qualities. He knows every melody, stop, tone and combination. Seating Himself in our consciousness, there come strains and harmonies never before heard by man, and our souls and bodies are quickened and healed, and all shout, "Alleluia: for the Lord God Omnipotent reigneth."

Was the organ at fault, then, when it gave forth discords and inharmonies? No, the combinations were wrong and there was lack of understanding on the part of the player. The tones and melodies were in the organ but the right combinations were needed to bring them out. To develop sweeter music we must get our combinations from above. We must have Christ at the Center. We must be able to say, with St. Paul, "It is no longer I that live, but Christ liveth in me." In other words, we must have Christ at the console before the music can be true.

Jesus said, "Ye shall know the Truth (right combinations), and the Truth shall make you free." The arrangement of the notes (the Truth) may be new, but the basic tones, the foundations, are old. The organ, like the Universe, will respond to us by corresponding to our combinations, or states of mind. If we are tuned to the Highest, as in the case of Jesus, then we shall bring out the grander, more sublime harmonies of life; and if we are tuned to the lowest, then we shall bring out the depressing and more destructive strains.

THE EMPTY HOUSE

In His parable on cleansing the consciousness, Jesus pointed out that the swept and garnished house of God should not be left vacant; it must be occupied against the reappearance of the former tenant. We read that "the unclean spirit, when he is gone out of the man, passeth through waterless places, seeking rest and findeth it not. Then he saith, I will return into my house whence I came out; and when he is come, he findeth it empty, swept and garnished. Then goeth he, and taketh with himself seven other spirits more evil than himself, and they enter in and dwell there; and the last state of that man becometh worse than the first."

Our greatest battle in life is not "against flesh and blood," but against the powers and principalities of darkness, and the evil suggestions so constantly pouring into us. In Jesus' day demon-possession was a very common ailment and it exacted a terrific toll. It manifested in so many different ways that demons were blamed for most anything that happened to a man. That is why Jesus gave the parable of the empty house. An undesirable tenant is expelled from a man's consciousness and thereafter "it roams through deserts in search of rest and can find none." (It was believed in those days that exorcised spirits inhabited the wilderness and forsaken ruins.)

Then it says, "I will go back to my house that I left; and it goes and finds it unoccupied, cleaned and all in order." The unclean spirit still calls it "my house" (setting forth the stubbornness of evil) and is delighted to find the place "empty, swept and garnished." No one better than himself had moved in so he repossesses the house. "Then it goes and gets seven other spirits more wicked than itself" (the seven other spirits represent the reinforcements of evil and a determined stand against subsequent eviction), "and they go in and live there, and in the end the man is worse off than before."

The empty house, however beautiful it may be, is always barren. It is a potential shelter for spiders, rats and other vermin, a latent hiding place for fugitives and thieves. It attracts the most undesirable and, like the unused ship at anchor, quickly goes to ruin. When evil is present, neutrality is impossible. The house that is not occupied by good will be occupied by evil. So the consciousness, if left empty, becomes a potential breeding place for all degrees of undesirable tenants and malignities, which eventually will destroy it.

The danger of lethargy and apathy is in its

state of emptiness. Sickness must be driven from the body by a change of consciousness. Otherwise it will return in a form worse than before. Buried grudges, hates, fears, worries, antagonisms and malign beliefs must be exorcised in the same way. As we tear down we must rebuild. For each displaced negative we must substitute a corresponding positive. It is not enough to deny place to these vampires that are exacting our very life blood; we must put something better in their place.

Our sword must be two-edged. As we let go of evil, we must take hold of Christ, not by pious show or empty phrases, but by allowing the Spirit to become active in us. We must not only possess Him but He must possess us. It is a choice between two masters—God or self, Christ or man, Divine Management or self management. Nature abhors a vacuum. She will not endure barrenness; she will not permit vacant spaces. Everything must be filled with something. The consciousness that is not presided over by a worthier tenant will be possessed by devils. When Christ comes to rule, the demons flee.

One of the chief charms of the Christian religion is its positiveness. Its Founder did not deal in postponements, negatives, or maybes. When the sick came to Him for healing, He did not say that He would see what He could do for them; or, that "perhaps" He could help them. He used affirmatives only. He spoke "as one having authority."

"Rise up and stand forth in the midst." "Stretch forth thy hand." "Arise, take up thy bed and walk." "I will, be thou clean." "Thy sins be forgiven thee." "Come forth, thou unclean spirit, out of this man." "Thy faith hath made thee whole." "Weep not; she is not dead, but sleepeth." "Be it unto thee even as thou wilt." "Thou dumb and deaf spirit, I command thee, come out of him, and enter no more into him." "Go in peace, thy faith hath saved thee." "Receive thy sight." "Lazarus, come forth." "Ye must be born again."

There wasn't a negative in Jesus' vocabulary nor His thought. There was always that absolute confidence and assurance which made Him victor over every difficulty.

To the father of the epileptic boy whose appeal to Jesus was, "If thou canst do anything, have compassion on us, and help us," He replied by quickening the father's faith. "If thou canst!" Jesus repeated the words with pained surprise. There was no need to stir God's Power into action. It is always in action. How long must He bear with these doubting and divided minds? "If thou canst!" Is anything too hard for God? Is not His Power unlimited? Then where is the limitation? In God or in man's capacity to receive? "All things are possible to him that believeth." The effect of Jesus' reply was immediate for instantly the father cried out: "Lord, I believe; help Thou mine unbelief."

To the people who are always asking what is to be accomplished by repeating affirmations and statements they do not believe, we reply: "Keep on repeating the words. Affirm them often enough and the healing of your unbelief will follow." It is said of some people that they tell a lie so often that they get to believe it themselves. Then why can't we tell a truth with the same effect? We can. If the constant repetition of a lie will culminate in the belief that it is true, then the constant repetition of Truth will culminate in an inward acceptance of Truth.

In other words, "the continued acknowledgment of a thought as true, plus sustained attention to it, creates a spiritual prototype. The prototype formed in the conscious mind is passed on to the subconscious mind. The subconscious is the connecting link between you and the divine substance . . . that . . . surrounds all life and out of which all life is created.

"It happens sometimes that an individual recognizing and using to some extent the positive side of the law loses sight of the negative side. Error-thinking has nearly the same potential power as Truth to create a prototype in the mind. If entertained and not destroyed, the error thought may be launched into the great sea of all-encompassing primordial essence. Then, because like produces like, the individual reaps a harvest of negation." Thus, "what you accept as truth becomes true—for you."

"I CAME NOT TO DESTROY, BUT TO FULFILL"

The trouble with most people who are trying to demonstrate Truth is that they are divided against themselves mentally. They are indecisive, fearful and uncertain. Jesus said, "I came not to destroy, but to fulfill." "I am come that ye might have life, and have it more abundantly." His mission was not to destroy but to construct; not to dissipate power but to conserve it. He had studied the reactions of the people to John the Baptist's scathing and fiery sermons on repentance and saw the need of following this purifying process with something constructive and positive. What John had broken He must mend. "What John had emptied He must fill." What John had destroyed He must rebuild. What John had injured He must heal. What John had started He must finish.

"I came not to destroy, but to fulfill." Jesus did not go about looking for the defects in people nor assailing them for their shortcomings. He saw the good in them and called it forth. He took unlettered, uncouth fishermen and molded them into great spiritual leaders. He transformed weak men into men of extraordinary power. He took little men and made them big. He took helpless men and made them strong.

Where there was sickness He healed it. Where there was ugliness He turned it into beauty. Where there was limitation He supplied abundance. Where there was bondage He gave freedom. Where there was death He gave life. Where there was sorrow He supplied joy.

Where there was hate He supplied love. Where there was ignorance He supplied wisdom. Where there was criticism He supplied Truth. Where there was weakness He supplied strength.

"I came not to destroy, but to fulfill." He filled every one so full of Himself that those who came in touch with them "took knowledge of them, that they had been with Jesus." To manifest perfection, we must keep a perfect model before us. We must look for the good and affirm the good at all times.

"And my God shall supply all your needs according to His riches in Christ Jesus in glory." Since God is so constantly pouring out His substance to us, there can be but one explanation for our failure to receive His gifts: we are not acting in manifestation with Him. Our minds are not harmonized with His Mind. Jesus' statement, "Apart from me ye can do nothing," means that without this union between the human mind and the Divine Mind absolute success is impossible.

There are many illustrations of this Truth in the Bible but the most outstanding is the case of Job. It was not until Job had surrendered himself to God that the Power began to operate in his behalf for that which he wanted. "I know," said he, "that thou canst do everything, and that no thought can be withholden from thee." That was Job's acknowledgment of the omnipresence of God, and the moment he recognized it that moment it began to operate for him. Having harmonized his mind with Divine Mind "the Lord gave Job twice as much as he had before."

Was Job's demonstration, then, unique? Not at all, for the same possibility is open to everyone who will bring his human mind into subjection to Divine Mind. To fail to do this, on the other hand, is to find our difficulties unchanged and our problems unsolved. We shall not only fail to demonstrate abundant living but we shall continue to be surrounded by trouble, worry, limitations and fear. The good things of life will pass us by.

SELFLESSNESS

How then shall we break this hateful bondage and get "twice as much" as we had before? There is only one way—to surrender the human mind to the Divine Mind. In other words, to become selfless. What do we mean by selflessness? We mean that habitual nonresistant attitude toward life which manifests itself in a perpetual state of mental and physical relaxation and balance at all times. It is the secret way to all spiritual achievement. It is surrendering to God, an active acceptance of the Higher Self as distinguished from the lower self.

It is God's business to provide for all our needs and it is our business to keep our thought channels unpolluted by the "vain imaginings" and discordant conditions of the outer world.

But how shall we attain this perfect balance represented by selflessness? There are several ways. First, we must eliminate all tension wherever we find it. Second, we must live, move, think and act without any undue waste of energy, and, thirdly, we must cultivate the expression of divine harmony and keep our thoughts off self and on God. This will mean watching ourselves to see that we are not using more energy than is necessary to accomplish a given purpose.

It will mean such things as keeping the mind and body relaxed at all times and under all circumstances, and particularly the muscles in the forehead, jaws, arms and legs; no matter what we may be doing or may have to do, we should always move quietly, calmly, easily and with just enough energy to accomplish what we have in mind. If we are driving our car, then we should not hold the wheel and floor board with energy needed to drive three or four cars. If we are writing, then we should not hold the pen or pencil as though some invisible force were trying to get it out of our hands. If it becomes necessary to move quickly, then we should never rush or hurry.

Particularly is this true when you oversleep in the morning. Take the penalty for being late but do not hurry. Take at least ten or fifteen minutes' time to get out of bed and you will not only live longer but your body will be stronger and serve you better. It is also better to go without a meal than to bolt your food. "Hurry is flurry, as distinguished from that calm and sure rapidity that is founded on mental poise. Hurry means tenseness in mind and in muscles." Rapid movement, if not executed easily, calmly and quietly, shocks the body and keeps it below par.

Among the many precepts in the Bible that cannot be denied are two which fit admirably into our present thought. The first was spoken

by Jesus and the second is from the Book of
Proverbs. "But I say unto you, Resist not him
that is evil: but whosoever smiteth thee on the
right cheek, turn to him the other also." "A
soft answer turneth away wrath."

The difference between the resistant and
nonresistant attitudes toward life are seen in
the parallel between a smile and a frown. When
one smiles he simply relaxes the muscles of
the face and when he frowns he contracts
them. When one frowns he is resistant and
when he smiles he is nonresistant.

The same truth applies to fear and faith,
worry and confidence, inferiority and superi-
ority, bondage and freedom, hate and love, sorrow and joy, wrong attitudes and right attitudes, condemnation and approbation, discord
and peace, self-consciousness and God-con-
sciousness.

Getting self out of the consciousness has the
same effect on the body as relaxing our grip
has on a rubber ball held tightly in the hand.
Relinquishing the body from the tension of
personal thought, it springs quickly back to the
image in which it was created. The terms receptivity and acceptance mean nothing more
than a relaxed state of being. To receive from

God we must be receptive (emptied of self),
and to be receptive we must be relaxed, and to
be relaxed we must be nonresistant.

"Selflessness," says M. Law, "involves a sub-
stitution of the Divine Will (all good) for the
selfish personal will. This process of substitu-
tion is consummated in the degree that we turn
away from the tyranny of the personal will,
whose objective is sense pleasure, to the
beneficent rule of the Impersonal Divine Will,
Whose concrete expression is happiness. No
longer resistant, we become still: we know
God. At least we understand that, while
pleasure can be bought in quantities, happiness
must be lived." When we cease to resist conditions, persons, places and things then we may
be said to be selfless.

Let us now turn momentarily to the me-
chanics of surrendering the human self for the
Divine Self. The Christ abides in us always.
He is "the first born of every creature." But
it is one thing to have a time-piece and quite
another thing to know the time. If we have a
watch and do not use it it is just as though
the watch did not exist. Jesus was asleep in
the little ship that was being tossed about in
the storm on the sea of Galilee but His Presence

there did not keep the ship from being battered about by the angry waves. It was only after His Power was recognized and awakened that the angry sea became still and the disciples' fears were calmed.

"Lo, I am with you always." The Christ is with us always, but until we recognize this fact and live by it our frail little craft will continue to be tossed about by every adverse wind that blows. "Beloved, now are we the sons of God, and it doth not yet appear what we shall be: but we know that, when He shall appear, we shall be like Him."

Notice the tense of this statement. "Now," it says; right now, this very minute we are sons. "When He shall appear"—not when we have shuffled off this mortal coil; not when we have entered paradise, nor some beautiful isle of somewhere; not when we have entered some imaginary purgatory or atoned for our sins. But when we have lifted the Christ up in our consciousness—then "we shall be like Him, for He only will be visible through us." As we retreat, the Christ advances. As we retire from the surface, the Christ takes our place. As we let go, the Christ takes hold.

Our whole duty therefore is to clear away

the obstructions so that the Christ can shine through. If someone offered us gold when we had our hands full of coppers, we would not consider it a hardship to drop the coppers in order to grasp the gold. God is constantly pouring out His blessings upon us; but many times we, in our ignorance, cling to the personal man instead of the Christ, and thus obscure the good that otherwise might be ours. It doesn't make any difference how brightly the sun may be shining; if we persist in walking on the shady side of the street because we have always taken that side, then we shall fail to receive the rich benefits of the sun's rays.

It is God's plan that everyone should be happy, healthy, prosperous and free. If we are not expressing these qualities, it is evidence that we are holding adverse thoughts that should be erased from our consciousness. We must dissolve the belief in evil before good can appear. We must give up the lesser that the greater may be manifest. When viewed in this light, surrender becomes a joyous adventure instead of a religious duty, and with each overcoming the way becomes easier and dominion increases.

The method of surrender most frequently

mentioned in the Bible is the one where the sacrifice is placed upon the altar and the fire is lighted by the priest. This is the trial-and-error method of the human mind, in which the individual tries to destroy his false beliefs and evil manifestations by personal will and the power of denial. It is like trying to lift ourselves by our boot straps and ends most often in frustration and defeat.

The other and by far the most successful method is where the offering is placed upon the altar and God sends the fire from heaven to consume it. "And when Solomon had made an end of praying, the fire came down from heaven, and consumed the offering, and the glory of the Lord filled the house"—(Solomon's consciousness). We, too, may use Solomon's method if we wish but we must give the problem wholly to God. The words "made an end of praying" mean, literally, when Solomon had learned to obey and trust God.

The fire from heaven will consume our offering and transmute our false beliefs into true beliefs and our false thoughts into true thoughts if we fully surrender them and trust Him. We must, of course, change our thoughts and keep them changed, but we must also keep in mind that it is the Father within that does the work and not we ourselves. In this realization, our demonstrations are easily and quickly made. The appearance of the New Man keeps pace with the disappearance of the old.

"The evolution of the soul begins with sacrifices on the material plane." If the true thought of God is to express through us, then we must eliminate from our consciousness all that is untrue.

Is your offering a false appetite, a desire of passion, that you cannot control, and which is detrimental to your health and welfare? Then you can offer it to God in words such as these: "Father, I lay this desire upon the altar of Your love. I let go of it freely and completely, and I trust You to transmute it into a desire for spiritual food, the greater good that You want me to have. I know that I shall be filled and satisfied by the living Word."

Is your offering one of personal relationships —a loved one, friend or personality whom you have sought to possess or bind too tightly in your thought? Would you like to release him and thus bring him closer to you in the Unity of the Spirit? Then you can accomplish this by using some such statement as this:

"Father, I know that — — — is Your child. I, as one having authority, strive to do your Will toward him and toward all of Your children who come into my life in any way; but I now relinquish all personal responsibility and all feeling of ownership toward him. I henceforth think of — — — as Your child and Yours alone, an agent sent to bless and to serve the whole world as Your beloved son. I know that all my dear ones, and all people everywhere, are Your children, and I have no personal claim upon any one of them. I give them into Your hands, and think of each one as Your free child, even as I am Your free child. I now place all feeling of personal relationship upon the altar and know that it is even now being dissolved and transmuted into the Eternal Love which is God."

In this way, the many thoughts, beliefs, feelings and impulses of the old man may be transmuted into the Christ Idea of the Perfect, Spiritual Man. All we need is to be willing to let go and let God do the work for us.

YOU CAN GET WHAT YOU
WANT IF YOU FIND IT
WITHIN YOURSELF

MEETING YOUR PROBLEMS
WHERE YOU ARE

THE WAY OUT OF ALL YOUR
DIFFICULTIES LIES IN
YOUR CONSCIOUSNESS

A glorious revelation awaits you when you discover that the Spiritual way of getting is by letting go and not holding on, and that the practical method of attracting what you want from the outer world is by first finding it within yourself. It is hard for the bargaining, material self to see any connection between an idea in the mind and an object in the world and yet they are but two ends of the same thing. The object, whatever it may be, is simply the mind in extension, an idea materialized. "Things which are seen were not made of things which do appear."

That is why Jesus told us to "Seek first the Kingdom of God," and why He taught his disciples to pray, "Our Father Which Art In Heaven." The only God we can ever know is the God of our own inner life, and the only place we can contact Him is within ourselves. "The Father Within, He doeth the works." This is the principle upon which Jesus built His matchless life and by which He did His mighty works, and it must be ours also; not just a human and limited sense of power, but a God-centered and Limitless one.

It is said that nine-tenths of the average man's life is lived in his environment (on the surface), and this is largely true. He is therefore the victim of his surroundings instead of being the master of them. Maybe you have wondered at times why it was so difficult to control your destiny and circumstances. The answer is very simple: you cannot control anything so long as you are controlled by it. Now remember that. It is one of the keys to the subject matter of this book.

YOU CANNOT CONTROL ANYTHING SO LONG AS YOU ARE CONTROLLED BY IT. Since your life and circumstances are made by the thoughts and impressions which are given free circulation through your mind, the obvious way to control them is to refuse to receive from the outside world those impressions which do not contribute to your highest good.

In the field of metaphysical science we classify all minds in one of two categories—the absorbent mind and the selective mind.

The absorbent mind is like a blotter; it not only absorbs most everything in its environment, but is under the influence of its environment at all times. The selective mind, on the other hand, rejects what it does not want and selects that which it does want. The selective mind molds its environment by discrimination and choice (taking what it wants), while the absorbent mind is molded by it. Thus one of the secrets in controlling environment is to be able to reject those impressions we do not want and to accept those which we do want.

The successful mind must be both repellent and absorptive. It must be both selective and receptive. The fundamental thing in spiritual work as in anything else is always receptivity, but it must be a guided receptivity. To keep life in perfect balance and to keep the good flowing in, the mind must not only be receptive to the higher and better things, it must also be impervious to the lower and baser things. The command to "Sit thou at my right hand, until I make thine enemies thy footstool," means that we must think with God (on the right side of the Law) until the power of the Infinite comes into expression in us and the difficulties in our lives have been removed.

"Consider the lilies of the field how they grow." How does a lily grow? Jesus says, by laborless activity. "They toil not neither do they spin." They grow by receptivity. As the bulb receives moisture and nourishment from the earth and air it produces the blossom on the stem. The bulb can give out only what it takes in. If it does not receive what Nature gives, it does not grow. If it does not begin with receptivity, it does not begin. The man who puts nothing into his prayer will take nothing out. The man who does not build his consciousness up to his ideal will never realize it. The stern law of life says: open yourself to God or perish—make room for the things above or you cannot have the things below. The genesis of every demonstration is receptivity and without receptivity there can be no response to anything. Our greatest good will come to us, then, only as we respond to the things which we consciously select.

THE INNER REALM IS THE REALM OF CAUSE

Probably the most difficult thing for the average person to understand is that the condition of his outer environment and circumstances depends entirely upon his innner relation to them. It is not uncommon to hear people say, "I have prayed and prayed and nothing happened." How do they know that nothing happened. How do they know but that their failure was the answer in disguise—their unbelief made manifest? Just because we pray for health when our consciousness is filled with sickness does not mean that we shall have health. "With what measure (mental equivalent—inner concept) ye mete, shall it be measured to you again." "As within so without."

The way to change your outer effects is to change the inner cause. The way to get what you want is to build a mental equivalent of that thing. To get rid of sickness, you must substitute a mental equivalent of health. That is, you must be more interested in health than in sickness. You must give more power to health than to sickness. It may take you months to build such a mental equivalent, but you will succeed if you keep at it, if you keep your thought alive with interest, and if you keep your new pattern clearly, definitely and steadily before you.

But maybe you do not understand the meaning of the term "mental equivalent." A mental equivalent is a formulated thought, or group of thoughts, representing the right desires you would like to have fulfilled in your life. It may be a mental equivalent for getting rid of something, or a mental equivalent for obtaining something. It does not make any difference what the nature of the mental equivalent may be, its one and only purpose is to change the mind. When the inner mind has been changed then the outer effects will change accordingly. In other words, we can only get rid of one thought and its manifestation by substituting another thought of an opposite nature. We supplant negative things by substituting right, constructive things.

Now, let us suppose that you have a mental equivalent of sickness which keeps you in ill health. How will you destroy this belief and its manifestation? There is just one way, by supplying a belief of an opposite nature. Think of your perfect self as you are in God. Realize that the Real Man is always well. Tell this to yourself over and over again. Keep your mind open to God and closed to all else. When the sick thought returns, discount it. Can it hold out against God? Is it stronger than God?

Drop it from your mind and change your thought into the new condition you are bringing about. Be steadfast in this practice and the true thought will automatically displace the sick thought, and the outer man will become well. Turn to God in every need and contingency of your daily life. Fix your gaze upon Him rather than upon the untoward setting you are trying to escape. Pray through your new mental equivalent in some such fashion as this:

"MY BODY IS PURE AND HOLY BECAUSE IT IS THE TEMPLE OF THE LIVING GOD."

"God has chosen my body to be His Holy Temple. 'Know ye not that your body is a temple of the Holy Spirit which is in you, which ye have from God? and ye are not your own.' As God's temple, my body is pure, free and perfect. It could not be otherwise, for God could not dwell in an unclean temple.

"From this day forward I shall think of my body as the habitation of the Almighty. No thought of disease, inharmony, impurity or imperfection shall enter my mind. Purity and wholeness of mind will keep my body whole and pure.

"As the temple of the Most High, my body is a place of loveliness and beauty, a place of vibrant activity and continuous renewal. It performs in Divine order and harmony all the righteous functions for which it was created. It is ever obedient to the Spirit of God indwelling in it, and it manifests only His Perfection. It is ageless, deathless, immortal, a living testimony to God's Power and Glory."

Now what have you done in this practice? You have changed the course of your life in the direction of your new belief. By changing your thought into the new pattern of Christ Perfection, you have not only destroyed the pattern for sickness, but you have laid the foundation for a new structure of health. By elevating your thought to God (the Truth of Being), you have opened yourself to an influx of Divine Power, Health and Wholeness, which, so long as you keep your thought changed into it, re-creates and makes you a new creature. "If thou return to the Almighty, thou shalt be built up." In Principle you do not have to worry about specific ills and ailments, but only to keep your thought changed into the new condition you are seeking to bring about.

You have now met the requirements of answered prayer and the Power will work for you according to your need.

But maybe you are one of those for whom nothing seems to go right. You are not sick but you have other difficulties, such as financial and domestic problems, worry, fear, etc., etc. It does not make any difference what your particular problem or problems may be, nor how many of them you may have, you always can build new mental equivalents, not only for the things you want to achieve but to destroy the patterns of those things which you do not want. The above outline is only a guide, a suggestion, as to what a new pattern or mental equivalent should be. Others will suggest themselves as special needs arise.

It may take considerable persistence to bring the new mental equivalent into manifestation, but the great Truth is, if you keep your mind changed into the new pattern your whole life and circumstances will be changed accordingly. Try it and see. All you need to do is to free yourself from the old beliefs and admit God. Change your attitude and God will change you —change your circumstances and the entire character of your life.

Then nothing evil can stand against you or

hurt you, for you are thinking, knowing, seeing and realizing God only. Then nothing but God can get into your life. You will immediately feel better and find yourself to be more powerful and self-confident. You will look and act like a new man, and others will see the change in you and tell you of it. Your faith will increase and a new capacity will be born in you. You will no longer look to others for your good, but you will look within yourself.

"If ye abide in me, ye shall then ask what ye will, and it shall be done unto you." If you keep your new pattern charged with interest, faith, love, confidence and thanksgiving, in the same way that the garage man charges the battery in your car with electricity; if you keep your thoughts clear and definite, and if you keep your mind open to God and closed to evil, then your mental equivalent will be demonstrated. Then God will give you what you want.

It is obvious, therefore, that the way to get what you want from the outer world is to consciously act upon the inner world, to build a new mental equivalent of the thing you desire and then draw it from that inner world. Many good prayers and affirmations remain unproductive simply because of some conflict or disbelief in the inner mind. "Not everyone that saith unto me, Lord, Lord, shall enter into the kingdom of Heaven; but he that doeth the will of my father which is in Heaven." Metaphysically interpreted, this means that prayer cannot be answered without the mental equivalent, or belief, of the thing asked for.

If a man would drink from the Fountain of Life he must bring his cup with him. He must bring the measure of that which he expects to take away. To receive from the Fountain of Life two things are necessary: First, we must be pure in heart (mind)—there must be nothing in the inner realm by which to divide or oppose the word that we speak. And, second, we must have but one Master, which is Truth.

It is "not that which goeth into the mouth defileth a man; but that which cometh out of the mouth, this defileth a man." It is not the adverse things that happen to us in the outer world that upset us and disturb our peace of mind, but what we think about them and how we react toward them. "Out of the heart (within) are the issues of life." This means that a man's life and circumstances always are like his consciousness. We talk much in spiritual work about demonstrating things but actually the only thing any one ever demonstrates is his consciousness. He always gets the conditions that belong to his consciousness and nothing else.

"Be not deceived; God is not mocked: for whatsoever a man soweth, that shall he also reap." This is the scriptural way of stating the great law of cause and effect, and it means simply that if you get demonstrations by any other means (will power, magnetism, hypnotism, etc., etc.) than by right of consciousness they will be only temporary. You have seen this law at work in the lives of many people who got things or took things which did not belong to them by right of consciousness. Their newly-acquired possessions remained with them but a short time and then disappeared. The moment their hands were removed from them they flew away. Why? Because the right of possession is determined by the law of consciousness. If a thing is related to our consciousness, then we can hold it indefinitely. If it is not related to our consciousness, then we can hold it only until some stronger force or circumstance takes it away from us.

Do you see now why it is that so many healings are only temporary? You "heal" a person of stomach trouble and he gets kidney trouble, "heal" him of kidney trouble and he gets heart trouble, "heal" him of heart trouble and he gets nervous trouble; you "heal" him of eye trouble and he gets ear trouble, and so on. These are not spiritual healings. They are what metaphysicians call "short term" cures. Without the consciousness to back them up they cannot last. There is nothing to hold them up. There is nothing to keep them in focus. You must realize, then, that the issues (conditions) of life are from within. If a person is healed by right of consciousness, then he is permanently healed. If he is not healed by right of consciousness, then the healing cannot last.

It doesn't make any difference whether a person uses material or spiritual means, or both, to get his healing. The basic thing always is consciousness. Did he get the consciousness of healing when the means were applied? To be whole in his body, a man must first be whole in his thought. To be free in the world, he must first be free in his consciousness. To be successful in the world, he must first be successful in his consciousness. To really own or hold a thing permanently, we must possess it by right of consciousness. Either we do have it by right of consciousness or we do not have it at all. The healings that are accomplished in the outer mind by superficial means are only temporary, while the healings that are accomplished by right of consciousness are eternal.

If we are going to maintain a permanent connection with God's supply, it is imperative that we look to and within our consciousness for all things at all times. Whatever the problem we must look within our consciousness for the answer. Whatever the need we must look to the Christ within us for its fulfillment. We must see to it that the within and the without are in harmonious relationship with each other at all times. That is, there must be no incongruity, friction nor antagonism between them at any time.

Our prayers will be answered when the inner mind no longer rejects the Truth which we assert. Our ills will drop out of manifestation when they are dropped out of our consciousness.

We do not have to straighten people out nor put things right in the outer world. We have to change our consciousness of them and our attitudes toward them. How do we do that? By letting "this Mind be in you, which was also in Christ Jesus." YOU HAVE THAT MIND NOW BUT IT CANNOT OPERATE FOR YOU UNTIL IT IS RECOGNIZED. That is why St. Paul said that we are to be transformed by the renewing of our minds, by replacing old concepts of disease and failure with the new concepts of health, freedom and success. When the inner mind knows the Truth, then the Truth shall make us free.

Please note that we said "inner mind" and not outer mind. The "inner mind" (consciousness) is awakened and changed by the constant repetition and steady contemplation of the spoken word (mental equivalent). Jesus said, "All things whatsoever ye pray and ask for, BELIEVE that ye receive them, and ye shall have them." The words "believe that ye receive them" means that when you inwardly accept (embody) what you ask it shall be forthcoming.

"Prayer is its own answer." But if you only partly believe when you pray then your prayer will remain unanswered. As the Bible says, it will be a cloud without rain, a desire without fulfillment.

There is an old saying that what cannot be

cured must be endured. We must either neutralize our troublesome and opposing thoughts and beliefs by thinking above them, replacing them with a better state of consciousness, or endure them. To the oft-repeated question, "Why is it necessary to say a prayer or make an affirmation more than once?" we reply that it would not be necessary if the one praying really embodied within himself all that he asked in the first prayer he made. If there were nothing to oppose or divide his spoken word, then he would get the same results in one prayer as in a hundred.

Thus the real purpose of repetition in prayer is to deepen the conviction and to increase the consciousness of the fulfillment of the thing asked.

When Jesus said "Believe that ye receive them," He meant that we were to get the clear realization that in Spirit we have the thing sought and we behold it coming into view. He always started with the assumption that His prayer was answered before He prayed. "Before they call, I will answer; and while they are yet speaking, I will hear." The prayer is made. It is answered. "It is done." GOD HAS

NO CHOICE BUT TO GIVE ME GOOD AND MY GOOD IS COMING TO ME NOW.

If I pray for health, then I must first get the clear realization that I have health in Spirit. If I pray for success, then I must first get the clear realization of success as a reality, and so I carry this vision to the point where failure no longer has any place in my consciousness. "With God (the clear realization that we already have in Spirit those things which we ask) all things are possible."

There is no problem too great; there is no difficulty that cannot be met; there is no obstruction that cannot be removed by the Presence and Power of God, if our concept of That Presence is strong enough and clear enough, and if the embodiment of our desire is complete. When the inner mind definitely accepts the new pattern (mental equivalent) as true, then the answer is assured.

A METAPHYSICAL ROSARY

The value of repetition in prayer is seen in the Roman Catholic custom of "saying the rosary." To the average Protestant this custom is childish, superstitious and non-sensical, but that is because he does not understand the psychology and power that underlies it. "What good can come from saying the same prayer over so many times," they ask. Well, let us get the answer direct from a Roman Catholic himself.

"Mary," said a young girl to a Roman Catholic friend, "why do you carry that rosary everywhere, and what possible good does it do to count those beads over and over?"

"Oh," answered Mary, "I never could make you understand what a comfort the rosary is to me. When I am tired, or blue, or discouraged about anything, or when I long very much for something that it seems impossible I shall ever get, I take my rosary and begin to pray. Before I have gone over half of its beads, everything is changed. The tired, discouraged feeling is gone; or, if I have been asking for something I long to have, it doesn't seem nearly so far away as before, and I know that if I don't get just what I ask for I'll get something better."*

"Heaven is not reached at a single bound; we build a ladder by which we rise from the

*ORISON SWETT MARDEN, The Victorious Attitude. Thomas Y. Crowell, Publishers.

lowly earth to the vaulted skies and mount to its summit round by round." Consciousness is not changed by a single prayer, but by a gradual unfoldment of the inner self.

In Isaiah we read, "Ye that make mention of the Lord, keep not silence, and give him no rest, till he establish." The vital things when you pray are to make sure that you get into the Higher Consciousness and that you hold firmly to the Truth. If you pray for supply, expect supply. Hold firmly to your pattern until supply is established. Keep your mind centered upon God's abundance and make no compromise with lack.

Accept nothing short of what you ask. Give the Lord (Law) no rest until He comes into manifestation as the good which you need. Keep on keeping on. Pray it through. Pray without ceasing. Let every act conform with the fulfillment of your desire. Let every word establish your pattern. Let every thought reinforce your prayer.

It isn't necessary to use a rosary made of glass or silver beads. The real rosary is the rosary of the heart. You can make one for yourself by stringing on the chain of your memory a series of new patterns or mental equivalents which represent the desires and aspirations of your soul, and if you repeat your statements not once, or twice a day, but dozens of times, and especially before going to sleep at night, you will be amazed at the good results.

Is it a problem you wish to solve; is it a misunderstanding you want to clear up; is it a difficulty you wish to overcome; is it an obstacle you want to remove; is it an illness you wish to heal; is it a sum of money you want to demonstrate—whatever it is that you need, make it a mental equivalent in your rosary. Affirm it. Change your mind into it. Contemplate it. Accept it. Pray for it. Work for it and your desire will be fulfilled.

The trouble with most people who are trying to improve their lives and to alter their circumstances is that they begin at the wrong end. Instead of changing the cause of imperfect manifestations within the mind by consciously and persistently acting upon it with the Truth, they try to change outer effects by patching them up. They forget that Life is a state of consciousness and that outer effects can be changed only as the self has been changed. Jesus said, "No man putteth a piece of new cloth unto an old garment for that which is put in to fill it up taketh from the garment, and the rent is made worse. Neither do men put new wine into old bottles, else the bottles break, and the wine runneth out, and the bottles perish; but they put new wine into new bottles, and both are preserved."

In saying that Jesus was teaching a lesson in spiritual unfoldment. If you try to change conditions without changing the consciousness back of them, you are trying the impossible. If you try to put new ideas into an old consciousness, you destroy the ideas. Life is new every instant but old thoughts cause it to appear old. Thus, the way to keep life new is to discard the old. When the old can no longer contain the new, then it must be transmuted into a greater good. Your success in spiritual work, then, depends not upon what you do in the without but upon what you do in the within, and how you relate yourself to the without.

"As a man thinketh in his heart so is he." It is your inner thoughts, attitudes and responses that make you what you are, and it is how you are related to the without that determines what you are to receive from the world.

Since all human troubles stem from man's ignorance of his true relationship to God, the first step in changing conditions is to see to it that all our thoughts are constructive and that all our relations are in perfect harmony. Jesus said, "Agree with thine adversary quickly." This means that you should see to it that you are in absolute harmony with everybody and everything at all times. Agree with your adversaries by refusing to be at cross purposes with any person, condition or thing. Meet all adverse thoughts with a positive, constructive and harmonious attitude. Allow no one and no thing to disturb your happiness or peace of mind under any circumstances. "Thou shalt worship the Lord thy God and Him only shalt thou serve."

Your greatest need is to have God acting with a full and complete expression in your life, and that need can be fulfilled only when you are in absolute harmony with the universe in which you live. It is the only way you can transcend present limitations.

It is a metaphysical law that whatever a man becomes conscious of that he will express throughout his entire world. What is involved in his consciousness will be evolved through his experience. What consciousness visions the mind will create, and what mind creates will be expressed in both body and affairs. Thus the conditions from which we suffer at any given moment are but the results of our recent thinking. The problems, troubles and ills of today are but the effects of wrong ideas held in mind yesterday; our circumstances of tomorrow are determined by what new ideas the mind may produce. As someone has said, "Immortality lies right in the next thing you do here. It is up to you to make good with eternity at the present moment. What you are thinking now counts."

When new ideas are introduced old ideas disappear. "Like attracts like." When the consciousness has been changed the condition will change. To try to change conditions, on the other hand, without changing the consciousness is like trying to change the picture on the screen without changing the film in the projector. It cannot be done.

HEALING

Healing is not creating a perfect condition in body or affairs; it is revealing a condition which already is perfect. Healing is not ac-

quiring something new, but an awareness of
something that already is. It is a revelation,
an exposition, a disclosure. People are not sick
and troubled because of circumstances over
which they have no control, but because they
have covered a perfect creation with imperfect beliefs. The age of the disease with which
you are afflicted has nothing to do with its
cure. The disease is only as old as your last
thought about it. This was proven by the beg-
gar at the Temple gate, who at the spoken word
suddenly jumped out of a crippled thought
pattern which had held him in bondage for
forty years. Changing his thought into a new
consciousness, he was instantly healed.

St. Paul said, "Power belongeth unto God."
Now ask yourself if there is anything in your
consciousness or body which is more powerful
than God. If you find that there is, then you
might just as well let God go and worship that
thing. Sickness, like trouble, is but the result
of subjectified thought—a belief in evil that is
stronger than the belief in God. It is a suggestion which consciously or unconsciously has
been allowed to fall into the subjective mind
and objectify as limitation.

What then is the antidote? To change the

thought from the negative condition to the positive condition, to neutralize the old troublesome thoughts and to send the right kind of thoughts down into the subjective mind. This does not mean parroting affirmations or holding thoughts in the outer mind, but getting the realization of the Truth contained in them so that the Good can work in our behalf.

When the gardener wishes to plant a seed he does not hold it in his hand, but he plants it in the earth. And so it is with spiritual seed. By staying the mind with deep feeling upon the Truth which the word symbolizes, we involve the right idea in consciousness, and then the consciousness evolves the idea as an effect in the body or in our affairs.

A professor rightly says, "Words in themselves mean nothing—the meanings go back to persons." When the seed is planted, the law must work and the effect must always be of like nature to its cause.

RESOLVE EVERYTHING INTO THOUGHTS

The first step in changing conditions is to resolve everything into thoughts and to keep the mind moving consistently and uninterruptedly toward the conditions to which we aspire. It makes no difference what outer appearances may be to the contrary, when the subjective recognition is right conditions also will be right. First we neutralize the belief in evil by seeing that it is neither person, place nor thing, but a subjectified thought, and then we invoke the right concept in the mind and hold to it until it is reproduced in experience.

As St. Paul said, "Put off the old man." Put off the limited and disintegrating ideas first and then put on the New (Perfect Idea), which is Christ. First, resolve everything—persons, problems, difficulties, diseases and things, into thoughts and then neutralize the evil (whatever it may be) by knowing that it is neither person, place nor thing, but an impersonal thought operating through your mind.

In Truth evil has no location. It does not belong to you nor to anybody else. It cannot operate through you without your permission. It cannot hurt you without your acceptance. Declare therefore that you do not believe in it and refuse to feed it by giving it your attention. Know that it is a false belief feeding your thoughts, and that it has no power to affect you beyond the power which you give it in your own mind. Know that it is purely mental; then mentally dissolve it.

When you continue with this practice until your consciousness is on the affirmative side of Good, and when you accept the blessing in the present, then nothing can hinder you from demonstrating what you desire.

It is not enough to make affirmations about your life and your needs. You must embody the truth contained in these affirmations by accepting them as your own. To express the Truth you must take it into your mind and hold it there until it forms in you a consciousness of itself. "Thou will keep him in perfect peace, whose mind is stayed on Thee."

You must harness the God Power to your needs in the same way that the electrician harnesses electricity to a motor, by making a connection and by keeping it firm. You must couple the Truth with your own life by incorporating It into your consciousness. First, you get a connection with the Power by lifting your thoughts to God, and, second, you keep it flowing (keep yourself perpetually sustained by the Power) by seeing, knowing and accepting nothing less than the Presence and Power of God in every person, place and thing.

"God is a very present help in trouble"—
IF, and this is the important point, if you have
travelled a path to His Presence. God will help
you if you have Him in the possessive case.
Your best prayer then will be: "Lo, I am with
you alway." The battle is God's, "Stand still,
and see the salvation of the Lord." "It is not
I, but God." Whatever your trouble or need
may be just place it lovingly in God's Hands.
Tell yourself over and over again, "God is
here. God is working in and for me. Nothing
can stand against God." Believe that—accept
it. "Before they call, I will answer; and while
they are yet speaking, I will hear."

God is. Not will be. Your health is not getting
better. You are WELL NOW. Your finances
are not improving. You are PROSPEROUS
NOW. Your difficulty is not diminishing. It is
DISSOLVED NOW. You are not growing
stronger. You are STRONG NOW. God is not
becoming this or that thing in your life. He is
that THING NOW. God is not growing up in
you. He is FULL GROWN NOW. God is not
trying to recover something which you have
lost. God HAS IT NOW. God is not trying to
remember something which you have for-
gotten. God already KNOWS. Spiritual evolu-

tion is not creating something but waking up to that which ALREADY IS.

"WHAT MUST I DO TO BE SAVED?"

The question, "What must I do to be saved?" is answered by St. Paul. "Be ye transformed by the renewing of your mind," and "Let this Mind be in you, which was also in Christ Jesus." In other words, change your consciousness from self to God. Since the mind is always creative and always working, it is always creating. "He that keepeth Israel neither slumbers nor sleeps."

To live is to think, and to think is to create. "All thinking is creative in some sense or form, and all that the mind creates will come forth sooner or later unless it is recreated before expression takes place." In the end each man becomes what he mentally creates, and the secret of becoming what he desires is by keeping his mind stayed upon the ideal he wishes to realize. Since the Law does not know or care what we use it for, and has no choice but to act, then the vision must be kept steady.

"What you continue to see in the within," says Christian D. Larson, "becomes a mental image. All such images act as models for thinking and the mind will create thoughts, states, conditions and actions that correspond exactly with those images. Every idea that comes into the mind becomes an image, and while it lasts millions of mental creations may be formed in the likeness of this idea. All these creations will appear in the person unless they are recreated before expression takes place. We therefore understand why it is so extremely important to have the right ideas about everything and why our ideals should be kept before the mind constantly."

Your consciousness then is the most important thing in your life. Indeed, it is your life. It is you. It is everything you are, have or ever hope to have. As your consciousness is so are you. As your consciousness goes so goes the man. On the material plane you bear the same relation to your consciousness as a cork bears to the water in a basin. If you let the cork represent yourself and your circumstances and the water your consciousness, you will see that the raising or lowering of the cork depends not upon the cork but upon the level of the water. If the water is disturbed, then the cork will be disturbed. If the water is peaceful, then the cork will be peaceful, and so forth. But the cork by and of itself is powerless to change its condition or position. Why? Because these are at all times determined by the level of the water (consciousness) and not by the cork.

A demonstration therefore would be nothing more than a change of consciousness, as when Jesus said, "I, if I be lifted up, will draw all men (manifestation) unto me." As the level of the cork is changed by changing the level of the water, so an evil condition is changed by a change of consciousness.

"In the world" (material-outer consciousness), said Jesus, "ye shall have tribulation; but be of good cheer; I have overcome the world." Actually the only problem there is in life is the problem of controlling consciousness, eliminating the weak spots in it, and embodying subjectively as many spiritual attributes as possible. When nothing seems to come back to us when we pray, we need to remind ourselves to, as Jesus said, "Judge not according to appearances."

As Harold Heard says: "Do not be disappointed when nothing happens, when no lucidity appears, no sense of significance, no great quiet. This process which is working on us works, or should work, first on the subconscious. What are we building up or having built up in us, is a foundation from the sea floor of the subconscious to the surface. Bag after bag of cement is poured in, and then it rises above the surface."

Thomas L. Masson likened consciousness to an apple "in which the possibility of decay is always present, in which indeed there are many soft spots; the problem is to keep it sound— not for any perverted or selfish purpose but for the innate priori intuitive longing for oneness with God."

And how does one keep his consciousness sound? By habitual practice of the Presence of God, by controlling his thoughts and by causing his mind to deal only with permanent things.

CHANGE THE SUBJECTIVE CAUSES

Solomon's statement, "As a man thinketh in his heart so is he," means that "Everything in the mind, body or environment of any man is the direct or indirect result of the subjective causations that are active in the being of that man." The weakness of most prayer is in its lack of depth. We pray with the outer (objective) mind but leave the inner (subjective) causes unchanged, and then wonder why there are no results from our prayers and why there is no improvement in our affairs. The trouble, of course, is that we pray with only half the mind. We change the outer thought and leave the inner cause unchanged. We ask for one thing with the conscious mind and at the same time prevent its coming with an opposing thought in the subconscious mind.

We are like the man who tried to purify the poisoned water of a stream by planting flowers on its banks. It is almost certain therefore when prayer fails to bring the desired results that it is because we have changed only part of the mind. If the subjective cause is wrong then the answer to the prayer can never be right, and, conversely, when the cause is right the answer will be right. St. James said, "Ye ask, and receive not, because ye ask amiss." As long as the subjective cause remains unchanged, as long as we feed it with our thoughts, then it is a certainty that the condition will remain unchanged. "Ye shall know the Truth, and the Truth shall make you free." It will make you free not so much by curing maladies as by removing the causes of maladies.

Evil could not exist unless we gave it a con-

sciousness to float in. Hence, evil persists only
because it has enough of our attention to keep
it alive. When our mind is centered in God, all
the power of the Universe is behind us; when it
is centered in self, it is all against us. To resist
evil therefore is to make it worse, and, by the
same token, to take life and substance away
from the very good we are seeking to materialize. St. Paul said, "Be not overcome of
evil, but overcome evil with good." We change
subjective causes by purifying our minds (refusing to recognize or give power to evil, and
we transform negative conditions by remaining
positive to God.

Do you see, then, where evil leaves off and
good begins? The dividing line is contained in
Jesus' statement. "Ye shall know the Truth, and
the Truth shall make you free." What truth?
The Truth that YOU ARE A SPIRITUAL
BEING CREATED IN THE IMAGE AND
LIKENESS OF GOD. On one side of this line
(thinking contrary to truth—away from God)
is bondage, sickness, limitation and trouble.
On the other side (thinking with truth—toward God) is freedom, Divine Wholeness,
plenty and peace. If you are a Spiritual Being,
as Jesus said, then you are in possession of all

the Divine Attributes now. They are in you as possibilities and will materialize when they are expressed. It is a fact therefore that the Real Self is never sick. Why not? Because sickness appears only on the surface. It is never in you but on you. Like all other trouble, it comes from a false conception of yourself. It is healed by a right conception.

We should turn within, then, for everything to the Great Power back of everything. We should turn to It as naturally and normally as we would turn to an earthly father, not only for the good and needful things of life, but for the solving of all our problems and for the healing of all our wounds. The Bible tells us that all created things were brought into being by the Word. "In the beginning was the Word, and the Word was with God, and the Word was God." The way out of every difficulty and the way into every blessing lies in the spoken word. The word is any definitely formulated thought, such as a prayer, affirmation or declaration of Truth. It is the Spirit-filled word, the Creative Power in action.

"Our words," says H. B. Jeffery, "if spoken in understanding are creative also; and they possess a reactionary influence that tends to raise the consciousness of man in regard to the Presence of God. That is really the object of prayer—to lift man's consciousness into greater awareness of the Presence of God; for when man is truly conscious of the Divine Spirit as present with him, he is conscious of every good and needful thing as also present with him and for him."

TRUE PRAYER

True prayer, according to Jesus, is not so much in asking God for things, as in lifting our minds above our needs so that we may be conscious of His Presence, in Whom all our needs are met and our desires fulfilled. Change in circumstances like change in the body begins with a change in mind. When our thoughts are lifted up to God, then He has promised to come to our aid, fulfilling the promise that "if ye turn unto Me, . . . I will turn unto you." The implication here is not that God has ever turned away from us, but that our return to Him makes it seem as though He had been away from us. Jesus said, "Lo, I am with you alway, even unto the end of the world;" and again, "The Kingdom of Heaven is at hand."

The Presence of God, meaning the presence

of everything good and desirable, is right here
with us—not near or far as to proximity of a
physical body, but by reason of our consciousness or unconsciousness of His Presence.

"The Divinity that shapes our ends is in ourselves, it is our very self." Then why the con-
tinual seeking after God with the outer mind,
which, as the Bible says, can never know Him?
Why all the begging, beseeching, reaching and
straining after the Infinite when He is nearer
than our breath and closer than our own hands
and feet? Why all the effort to tell the ALL-
KNOWING Spirit what He already knows?
Did not Jesus say that "Your Father knoweth
what things ye have need of, before ye ask
Him." Then why treat Him as though He were
ignorant? Why inform Him of the things that
He already knows? Do not the scriptures tell
us that, "Before they call, I will answer; and
while they are yet speaking, I will hear." We
do not have to beg God to supply our wants,
but only to keep our minds above those wants
and on Him, so that His supply can get through.

The great medium of self-realization is self-
surrender. "He that would find his life must
lose it." To function in a new plane of consciousness, we must die to the old. To partici-

pate in a Higher Life, we must surrender the lower. To rise to health, we must die to sickness. To rise to success, we must die to failure. Self consciousness must surrender to God Consciousness. Me consciousness must surrender to "I" Consciousness. The human must surrender to the Divine. Before the Christ Self can be realized, the human self must be denied. That which is must surrender to that which ought to be. The circumference must surrender to the Center. In order to find ourselves we must lose ourselves in Something Bigger than ourselves.

Jesus said, "Leave all and follow me." There is a vast difference, you see, between being a Christian and following Christ. It is the difference between recognition and realization, between mental assent and practice. To follow Christ we must make this transition from natural life to Spiritual Life. We must do it by turning the soul away from its natural associations and preoccupation with the outer world and by turning it in a wholly new direction, toward the Central living part of our being, which is God. That is what prayer is for. It is changing our thought and feeling from self to God. It is the filament in the electric light globe surrendering to electricity, the cocoon surrendering to the butterfly, the egg surrendering to the chick, the seed surrendering to earth and air, the sick man surrendering to the doctor, the personality surrendering to individuality, the partial life surrendering to Whole Life—prayer is your whole being surrendering to God.

If Jesus were here in the flesh teaching us today He would probably say: Be what you want in your consciousness and you will attract it from the outer world. The way to change the without is to change the within. The way to get is to give. The way to climb is to let go. The way to control circumstances it to control your thoughts. The way to attract better circumstances is to make more of yourself. The way to solve problems is to keep them out of your thoughts and your mind on God. The way to acquire the things you want is to find them within yourself. The way to increase your income is to increase your consciousness of supply. The way to surmount difficulties is to change your attitude toward them. The way to find God is to lose yourself. The way to make more of your opportunities is to make more of yourself. The way to get a bigger job is to be a bigger man. The way to get better friends is to be a better friend.

The way to put yourself on the receiving end of God's Love is to keep all opposing thoughts out of your mind. The way to be true to God is to be true to yourself and to your fellow man.

SEEK THE ABOVENESS OF LIFE

"If ye be risen with Christ (if you have a true relationship with Him), then seek those things which are above," where Christ is. Seek the aboveness of life. Seek it by letting go of all suspicious, unmerciful and hateful states of mind. Seek it by giving up all criticism, antagonism, bitterness, envy and jealousy. Seek it by refusing to entertain ill-will, grudges and resentments, and by refusing to be occupied with anything that is unlike God.

Center yourself in God and God will center Himself in you. Get that within you which is above you and that which is around you cannot trouble you. Get your Center right and your circumference will be right also. Give your best to others and they will give their best to you. Look for the best in others and others will do their best for you. Have faith in everybody and everybody will have faith in you. Seek the best everywhere and you will meet the best wherever you are. Make the best of everything and you will attract the best of everything. Love everybody and everybody will love you. Live in the present and your worries will disappear.

St. Paul said, "I can do all things through Christ which strengtheneth me." Notice the words "THROUGH CHRIST." Your ability to be successful in life depends not upon your opinions, but upon your consciousness. DO YOU HAVE THE MIND OF CHRIST? If you have It, then your within and your without are in perfect harmony, and the resources of Heaven are on your side. If you do not have it, then your Heaven is in reverse—instead of implementing your thought and life, the within and the without pull against each other and offer resistance to it. You are, in the vernacular of the day, "off the beam" or "out of tune." If Christ goes out of your life then everything desirable goes out with Him—your life is separated from its Source.

Isaiah sensed this universal tendency toward limp thinking (thinking without God) when he said, "The peg driven in so firmly shall be wrenched out and give way, till everything that hung on it shall come down." The whole trouble, you see, is that we have hung our lives and affairs on the wrong peg—the unreliable and impermanent peg of the human mind. Thus when trouble comes, or the bottom drops from under us, we have nothing to hold us up, nothing to hold us together. Without the Mind of Christ we are like the moon, shining by reflected light. We are like the branch separated from the vine and soon exhaust the little life we have.

Then how shall we meet this problem? By driving in a new peg—by entering a new state of consciousness. As St. Paul says, "Enlarge the border of your tent—launch out into deeper waters." It makes no difference how great or how extensive your needs or wants may be, the way to get more than you now have is to get a larger consciousness of it. "Prove me (Christ) now herewith, saith the Lord of Hosts, and see if I will not pour out a blessing, that there shall not be room enough to receive it." To release the blessings of Heaven you must enter into the consciousness of Heaven. Get the consciousness of Heaven (the Whole) first and then all these things shall be added unto you.

To the consciousness of health you automatically express health in your body. To the consciousness of supply you automatically express supply in your affairs. You do not demonstrate health and supply. You simply appropriate and express those things which already are there. In the new state of consciousness, you no longer affirm the Truth but accept it. Then everything automatically becomes new; and you cry, "Whereas before I was blind, now I can see." Having the Mind of Christ, God now sees through your eyes and you see perfectly.

Just as it is impossible to change the shape of the air in a room until the shape of the room has been changed, so it is impossible to change circumstances until the consciousness has been changed. Man works from the outside in, while God works from the inside out. Jesus' guarantee of freedom was based absolutely upon man's knowledge (consciousness) of Truth. "Ye shall know the Truth" (be conscious of it), He said, "and the Truth shall make you free." It shall make you free (work in your behalf) when, and only when you have emptied your mind of everything that is untrue or inimical to it.

Why is this so? Because you get in experience only what you have in your consciousness. "As within so without." The within is your formulated thought and the without is your experience of it. Prosperous thought means prosperous experience. Poverty thought means limitation and suffering.

It is profitless therefore to pray for benefits, blessings and gifts if at the same time we are thinking thoughts, holding attitudes and doing things which are frustrating our own ends. God does not withhold from us, as Jesus pointed out, but we withhold from ourselves. We do it by our divided beliefs, our wrong attitudes and our negative feelings. Yes, we actually barricade ourselves against our own acceptance of His Gifts. That is why St. John told us to confess our sins. "If we confess our sins" (empty them out), he says, "He is faithful and just to forgive us our sins, and to cleanse us from all unrighteousness."

What does this mean? It means that "confession is good for the soul." As we cleanse our minds of all opposing and un-godlike thoughts, then we shall find that the benefits we sought were already here. They were waiting for us even before we thought of them. They were given before we asked.

The scriptural pronouncement that "Now it is high time to wake out of sleep" means that the belief in separation from God is a dream from which we must awake if we are to return to the Father's House (Source of Life). As one awakes from a bad dream, so the mind awakes from the belief in a power opposed to God. "We cast off the works of darkness, and . . . put on the armor of light" when we realize that evil is not a reality but a false belief masquerading as Truth. The invitation to "seek those things which are above," to "come up higher," to "arise and shine," to "lift up your hearts," etc., etc., are all invitations to recognize the Highest, seek the Highest, practice the Highest and give hospitality to the Highest.

The highest spiritual practice is the practice of the Presence of God. The highest form of prayer is uplifted thought. The highest form of faith is absolute dependence upon our consciousness for all things at all times. The highest form of Spiritual communion is our realization of our unity with the Whole. The highest form of mental action is to let the

Father Within do the works through us. The highest form of thinking is to think with the Mind of Christ.

The highest form of demonstration is the embodiment of the Kingdom of God in our thought. The highest form of healing is the appropriation of a new consciousness within. The highest form of meditation is detachment and spiritual relaxation. The highest form of freedom is conformity to spiritual Law. The highest form of mentality is the Mind of Christ. The highest form of acceptance is thanksgiving. The highest form of spiritual attainment is self-forgetfulness. The highest form of co-operation is transparency of thought. The highest form of consciousness is the consciousness of the Indwelling I AM.

When Jesus said that the younger son took his journey into a far country, He meant that he had taken from himself the most valuable thing in his life—his contact with God. In running away from God he had run away from himself. He had lost his awareness of Good and was now wasting his substance in riotous living. He was wasting it because there was no longer anything to hold it together. He was out of touch with his Source. Having separated his mind from God's Mind, he had separated himself from everything desirable and worth while in his life. He had shifted the gravity of his thought from Center to circumference, from God to self, and this was one of the worst sins he could have committed. It was one of the worst because it took the whole man with it. Separating his thought from God he now worked against the Kingdom instead of with it. He had entered the deplorable state to which Emerson referred when he said, "Self consciousness is the fall of man."

It is obvious therefore that both heaven and hell are states of mind. If Heaven is within you as Jesus said, then hell must be in the same place. Thus what we call Heaven and hell are just different relationships to God. If we obey the laws of Spirit, then we have Heaven, and if we disobey we have hell. In Christ Consciousness we have Heaven while in self consciousness we have hell. Both are states of mind and both are present conditions. As man falls away from God in his thought God moves away from man. God moves away not in the sense that he leaves man but because man's relationship to Him is weak. He is looking through the wrong end of the telescope, so to speak, and God seems far away. St. Paul referred to this low state of visibility as seeing "through a glass darkly."

There still are countless millions of people looking for Heaven or hell in some other time or place, but just where this other place could be no one seems to know. Jesus said, "NOW is the accepted time," "NOW is the day of salvation." "The Kingdom of God IS (is means now, present tense) within you." "NOW are we the sons of God." Isn't it clear therefore that Heaven and hell are not rewards or punishments to come after death, but states of mind that are begun here and carried over in our consciousness to the next plane of existence?

Then why postpone your good until some future time? Why perpetuate the same old mistakes from one day to another? The Truth is that you will get in the next life just exactly what you take out of this one. Why? Because "Life is a state of consciousness." Life hereafter is but a continuation of the life here. There is only one Life and that is eternal.

The life you are now living is the only life you will ever have. What you get over there will be what you take from over here. That is why Jesus said, "Lay up for yourselves treasures in Heaven—in mind. If you take Heaven out of this life then you will find Heaven in your continuing life. It makes no difference where you are at any given time, the place in which you find yourself always will match your mental state. The Kingdom of God always will work for you or against you according to your consciousness of it. The old saying "shrouds have no pockets" means that the only things you will take with you are the things you have in your consciousness. To get more in the outer world you must have more in the inner world.

MISSING THE MARK

The English word "sin" is from the Anglo-Saxon word "syn," meaning to miss the mark or to fall short. It is a term used in archery to indicate the misdirection or misplacement of the arrow. Instead of hitting the center (bull's eye), it falls upon some portion of the circumference, and this is a syn, or missing the mark. The syn in archery is misplacing the arrow and the sin in life is misplacing the "I," or identifying it with the lower, personal self and the created things of the world, thus becoming a sinner "who changeth the Truth of God into a lie, and worshiped and served the creature more than the Creator."

If "power belongeth unto God," as St. Paul said, then to give power to evil, problems, persons, difficulties and things is to sin, to miss the mark, to misplace the "I," to misappropriate power and to become a prodigal. That is what had happened to the young man in the story. Having disrupted his life by the displacement of his "I," he was away from the Kingdom of God and a wanderer in a "far country." "And no man gave unto him" because no one can give unto him but himself.

Jesus painted this picture just as black as possible to show us that all our troubles come from a sense of separation and misdirected energy. No one could change this distressing situation in which the son found himself but the son himself. "There are no gods to say us nay, for we are the life we live." The prodigal must live on in the pig pens until he and the Father are reunited. He must continue in his distress until he stops thinking of himself as a prodigal and thinks of himself as a son. The door of the Father's House always is open but each man must enter for himself. Since God cannot enter discord, then we must enter harmony. Since we cannot contract the Divine, we must expand the human.

Whenever Jesus used the "I AM" He always identified It with His individuality, the Supreme Self, to which all other things in life are secondary. "I, if I be lifted up, will draw all men (manifestation) unto me." When the "I" is lifted up in consciousness, that is when we identify It with the divine "I AM," when we recognize it to be the ruling principle in our lives and superior to and above all else, then individuality becomes masterful and strong. We lift ourselves up, so to speak, and place ourselves where we belong—in the Father's House.

Most teachers stress the importance of keeping the "I" in place, but few of them tell you why. There are two very definite reasons. First, the "I AM" is the very center and source of all action which takes place in your world. If you wish to control conditions (get above them) and make your life what it ought to be, then you must act and think from the source of power and initiative. You must act and think, not with the human mind as a body or personality, but with the Christ Mind as a soul and individuality. You must act and think not as John Doe, but as the "I AM." You must know that the "I AM" is you, and the more you do this the more power you will have to direct and control your life.

The second reason is that the "I AM" occupies the entire field of consciousness and controls all the forces in the human system. The individuality means the Real Man as distinguished from the personality. "The I AM, from the Universal standpoint, means God; and from the individual, means the Real Man." The individuality is the Spirit of man and the personality is the use he makes of it. In the average person, the "I AM" is identified with the personality or body, thus removing them from his control. Submerged in human beliefs and limitations, and receiving no direction from the Source of Being, he is the victim of his circumstances instead of being the master of them. Living on the lower plane where evil has power to affect him, there is no escape from his ills. He is in constant bondage to his own beliefs and ideas.

What then is the remedy? To elevate the thought to God, to recognize that the "I AM" is the "one and only Real Mind or Power in the Universe," and to know that the "I AM" is you. When you keep your thoughts centered in the universal "I AM," then you bring them into harmony with the Creative thought of the universe. Thinking and acting from the Source of Power, you will be above and superior to everything in your world. You will be master of every situation and victor over every ill.

Would you like a simple method of restoring the "I" to its rightful place? Then enter the silence for a few minutes every day (See the author's book—"The Creative Silence") and contemplate the "I AM." Try to realize that you, the individuality, are not only above your world (body, mind and affairs), but in a very definite way distinct from it. "Come ye apart and be ye separate," said Jesus. The real purpose in isolating your "I AM" from the rest of your organized existence is to build up a deep consciousness of your own individuality (I AM), and to cause you to think always of the Universal "I AM" when you think of yourself. If you are faithful in this practice, then gradually all your thoughts, actions and supply will come directly from the "I AM," or Source of Life. Being above your mind, you will control everything in your body.

Now please do not confuse this method of

isolating the "I AM" with the unholy practice of denying evil. "There is nothing in all my holy mountain to be destroyed." The denial of evil is an affirmation of evil. It is unscientific. There is nothing we can do about our false beliefs except to supplant them with the right beliefs. To confess our sins does not mean to deny them, but to let them go, to refuse to express them, to refuse to give them power. They are forgiven when we stop sinning.

We do not have to erase a false belief from the mind before the right belief can be planted. We do not have to shovel the darkness out of a room before the light comes in. We do not have to scoop the emptiness out of the bath tub before it can be filled with water. "We do not have to remove that which is nothing before we can introduce something." To deny evil is to establish in the mind the very evil we are trying to deny. It is obvious therefore that denials are nothing but a waste of time. They are like opiates which delay for the time being the final reckoning.

To the questions "Why did this have to happen to me?" "Why do I have so much trouble?" etc., etc., there can be but one answer—misdirected energy. In fact, there is no other cause for trouble. When the "I" is misplaced (identified with outer circumstances instead of inner reality), as in the case of the prodigal son, we produce conditions of emptiness (absence of good), which we call evil. That is what evil means—absence of good. When the Divine Energy is misdirected it does not go where it should. Instead of producing conditions of good as in the case of directed energy it produces states of evil. If the mental forms are wrong then the outer effects cannot be right.

The energy that manifests as sickness and trouble in no way differs from the energy that manifests as health and peace. It is not the energy that is at fault, but the thought that directs it into good channels or bad.

We should remember this therefore when engaged in building new mental equivalents or in making affirmations of Truth. If an affirmation is to culminate in realization then it must be built upon absolute Truth. What do we mean by absolute Truth? We mean the positive acceptance of the Ideal (fulfillment of our desire) in the present moment. If one were seeking health, for instance, he would not say, "I am improving" or "I am getting better," but "I am well." Why? Because the first two statements are relative truths implying change and growth, while the last is absolute, the mental acceptance of that which is.

But why should one say that he is well when he is not? Because the expression of the absolute Truth in the mind causes it to speed up the manifestation of Truth in the body, while relative truths slow down the action of the mind and prolong the illness. It is perfectly proper therefore to declare that you are well because the Inner Self, the Real Man, the "I AM," or individuality, is always well.

Jesus said, "By thy words thou shalt be justified, and by thy words thou shalt be condemned." The whole problem, you see, is a matter of words and what you put into them. If you are really serious about keeping your "I" in place (keeping your energy in constructive channels), so that all the elements and powers of your being work for the things you want, then you must watch your thoughts and try always to speak words of Absolute Truth.

Instead of misplacing the "I" by identifying it with the undesirable, by saying, "I am weak," "I am poor," "I am sick," "I am getting old," etc., etc., you should keep it moving toward the Ideal by thinking thoughts and speak-

ing words of Absolute Truth: "I am strong,"
"I am rich," "I am well," "I am young." In the
Absolute these latter statements are all true
and they can be verified by creating within
yourself mental equivalents that can produce
them in your experience.

The hidden power in words is in the consciousness in which they are spoken. This
power may be good or evil. It may attract what
you want or do not want. It may promote your
good or retard it, depending upon the feeling
you put into your words. The counterpart of
the statement that "As a man thinketh within
his heart so is he," is, As a man feeleth within
his heart so is he. It is always the feeling (inner conviction) in the words that determines
the direction of the Power; therefore when you
feel fulfillment in your words, you cause the
"I AM" to create fulfillment in your affairs,
while if you express uncertainty in your words
then you delay fulfillment in the outer world.

Let us recognize, then, that the real remedy
for bad conditions is to return the "I" to the
Father from whence It came as when St. Paul
said, "It is no longer I that live but Christ
liveth in me." The word salvation from the
Greek "soteria" means a safe return to the

Father's House, and this is accomplished by centering our thought in God and by recognizing that He is the only Presence and Power in our lives. We let our "I" go again unto the Father when we recognize and accept Him as the ALL-IN-ALL. We build power within ourselves when we refuse to give power to persons, places, circumstances, conditions and things.

FORMULA FOR RESTORATION OF THE "I"

"Thine, oh Lord, is the greatness, and the power, and the glory, and the victory, and the majesty, for all that is in the heaven and in the earth is Thine; Thine is the Kingdom, oh God, and Thou art exalted as head above all. Both riches and honor come of Thee, and Thou reignest over all; and in Thine hand is power and might; and in Thine hand is to make great, and to give strength unto all. Now, therefore, our God, we thank Thee, and praise Thy glorious name."

"ALL THINGS BECOME NEW"

"Old things are passed away; behold, all things are become new." It is the new that is called for in religion today. And the new does not necessarily mean an abolition of the old. "New styles of dress by no means do away with clothes. New styles of type do not do away with printing. New styles of architecture do not destroy the building of homes. They make living more comfortable. New methods of husbandry do not destroy vineyards and orchards but more surely establish them. Governments are not destroyed by reforms, but amendments preserve them. Jesus' ideas were revolutionary to His age, as the new always is, but He said: "I am come not to destroy, but to fulfill." How? By a new consciousness of life.

If the Truth is to make us free as Jesus said, then it must be adapted to life, and life is ever changing. Closed minds fear changes while open minds welcome them. "Multitudes look upon the church as a ship transporting them to Heaven, and every change is of the nature of a leak that threatens the safety of the ship." Such people do not realize that the Christian religion is dynamic and not static. They stagnate for want of the new, because they are unwilling to combine it with the old.

If the church of the future is to be a healing

church as was intended by its Founder, and if it is to function as a living organism in the lives of its members, then it must appeal to the undiscovered part of man, to the vast, hidden and latent forces within him which he has never been able to get hold of by himself. It must be so integrated with his mind and heart that it will give new meaning and power to his life. It must unlock the new forces and resources which will enlarge him. It must change its "Come to Jesus" type of theology for the "Let Christ be formed in you" variety. It must stop generating morbidity, guilt, inferiority, inadequacy, sinfulness, solemnity, pessimism, hopelessness, poverty, doubt, resignation to life as it appears, fear of a distant God, and start cultivating health, well being, poise, prosperity, happiness, buoyancy, confidence, courage, vision, faith and power.

One of the chief functions of the regenerated church must be to put man in possession of himself, physically, mentally, morally and spiritually—to discover a new man in the old one, and to make him dominant. It must spend more time redeeming him from the problems, worries and ills of life and less time to the bolstering of ecclesiastical institutions. It must give more thought to the cultivation of God Consciousness and less thought to church consciousness, more attention to applied religion and less time to theoretical religion, more effort to cooperation and less to competition, more emphasis on the Kingdom of God and less upon denominations. It must give more time to teaching and serving others and less time to oratory and self-centered activity. It must have more worship in the spirit and less in the letter, more emphasis upon the present and less upon the future.

Let every cleric choose therefore whom he will serve, a Living Christ or a dead Lord. The church does not need more power and equipment. It needs more and a better use of the power and equipment it already has. It needs less formal assent and more personal acceptance, less talking and more living, less theory and more practice. It needs the brighter and more joyous side of life.

HARNESSING THE POWER

"There is a river the streams whereof make glad the city of God." There is a stream of relentless power running through every man's life which has its Source in God. Its outlet is the mental and emotional energy of thought, will, imagination and desire. To allow this power to run unharnessed, unchecked and unguided, is the basic cause for all the evil and suffering on the earth. To control it, on the other hand, is the secret of all happy and successful living. "He that ruleth his spirit is greater than he that taketh a city."

Since all inner urges tend toward outward expression, the obvious way to control conditions is to control the power that makes them. And how do we do this? By disciplining our desires and by getting a new hold on life. "When we turn our faces toward the Light, and contemplate our highest conception of Divine Perfection, we become opened to receive an influx of Divine Life and Power. If, however, we contemplate our sins and failures, and bemoan our sinful propensities, we shut ourselves off from the Life of God, and open ourselves more fully to the very things we so strongly desire to overcome."

Buddha tried to solve the problem of desire by making man desireless. But you cannot solve the problems of life by contracting life, any more than you can cure engine trouble in your car by getting rid of the engine. The remedy lies not in contraction but in expansion. We must have something within us that is bigger than anything outside us. The way to eliminate destructive desires is to replace them with constructive desires.

How, then, shall we harness this power, conserve this energy, control these urges and discipline our desires? How shall we develop the mental and spiritual equipment which will enable us to stand firm in the midst of the turbulent river with nothing physical to cling to? How shall we develop automatic spiritual reflexes with which to meet the dangers that beset our paths and the cross currents that encompass us on every side? By surrendering our lives to Christ and by lifting our minds to His mind. In the words of St. Paul, "I desire that ye faint not . . . that Christ may dwell in your hearts by faith; that ye, being rooted and grounded in love . . . be filled with all the fullness of God . . . according to the Power that worketh in us."

The way to get a new hold on life is to break with both past and future and to live in the present. In other words, to live in balance. David Seabury says: "Disease is a loss of balance in part or in all of the organism. It may begin in the spirit and end in bodily disintegration. It may start from physical causes and react upon the psyche. But always it is a loss of balance in one's basic being. Too little or too much emotion at once records itself in the endocrine system. Neither inhibition nor wild release of feeling tends to health. . . . Too much or too little food, exercise, sleep; indeed too much or too little of anything destroys health. Only by achieving a psychical and physical equilibrium on and between each plane of life is a man's vigor maintained."

The reason why it is important to train ourselves to live in balance (in the present), is because that is the only time in which we can participate in the blessings of God. It is the only time in which Spirit functions. Lot's wife crystallized when she looked back, and many another person has crystallized in looking forward, in crossing bridges and in anticipating troubles before coming to them. The only safe mental attitude therefore is to face forward in the present, to enjoy the blessings which are here and to prepare for those which lie ahead. To get a new hold upon life, we must neither reflect upon the reverses nor the successes of the past, but see and accept the new blessings of the present. We can do this by clipping off each day as it passes and by filling our minds with new thoughts, new interests, new ideals.

Dr. William Osler, the world-famous surgeon, said, "The load of Tomorrow, added to that of Yesterday, carried Today, makes the strongest falter. We must learn to shut off the future as tightly as the past." Jesus said: "Sufficient unto the day is the evil thereof."

By constantly raising our thoughts to God and by surrendering our wills to His Will, we build within ourselves spiritual reflexes which automatically come to our aid when we need them. We also build a sort of invisible dam which not only insulates us against evil but gives us greater control of our own power. The words and affirmations we use are important only as scaffolding to hold the thought in place until the Spiritual substance sets. Then when all the props are taken away the words which formed in us a consciousness of themselves stand alone "to do battle against whatever might come to destroy it."

There are many theories on the subject of Spiritual Power and as many methods for applying it, but the truth is that none of us will ever have more power than our detachment and self-forgetfulness provide. Practical religion is really nothing more than getting rid of the obstructions so that the Great Force can get through us. We often speak of "our power," but it really is not our power at all; it is merely that, through confidence, we free ourselves to become good channels through which the power can flow.

Our main business is with God and our chief responsibility is to maintain a firm connection with His Power. Church membership is important but it will not save us. God is in all churches and all religions, and nothing else matters. Denominations and forms are simply different ways of seeing and worshiping One God. The important thing in religion is practicing the Presence of God and turning to that Presence for every need. The advice of the Master is to accept nothing less, and to be satisfied with nothing less than perfection. Do all you can spiritually and leave the rest to Him.

The only time he does not work in our behalf (for what we need) is when we are unconscious of His Presence, or away from His House. The firmest contact with God is gained through a change of thought and self-forgetfulness. "Be absent from the body, and present with the

Lord." You can always surmount an obstacle by an attitude. You can always get what you need by detaching yourself from it—by making it of no importance in your thought.

RUNAWAYS

There is nothing in the parable to indicate why the younger son left home to go into the "far country" unless it was the churlish attitude, jealousy and critical aloofness of the elder brother. No doubt he, like many another person finding it impossible to live with his problem and solve it where he was, decided to run away. It is surprising how many people take this course when under stress. Their first impulse when some criticism, disagreement or trouble comes is to run away, to quit the place where they are, and to drop everybody and everything in the belief that things in some other place will be much better, that conditions will be more agreeable and that people will be much nicer and easier to get along with.

The psychiatrist has a name for this kind of behavior but we know that it is one of the chief causes of so much regret, disappointment, frustration and failure in human life. It stems from the old belief that "hills are green far away."

In the army those who run away from their tasks are called deserters, or AWOL (absent without leave). In time of war they are court-martialed, and shot, or made to serve out stiff prison sentences at hard labor. But those who are engaged in warfare between good and evil consider that they can be AWOL from their battle stations (slight their daily study and practice) at their own convenience and that no one should censure them at any time. They do not know that spiritual work is cumulative and that each time they skip a meditation they loose much momentum. They simply are on "self-appointed prolonged vacation," or shall we say "detached service?" Actually, such persons should be designated as casualties or as "missing in action."

In the old days when the problems of life overwhelmed men they sought refuge in convents and monasteries. It was an attempt to run away from life, to shirk responsibility. It was so much easier to say prayers and live in poverty than to face life and overcome it. These men were runaways and deserters. They no longer had the heart and will to seek for themselves. Life had ceased to be an adventure for them and they sought security in detachment. They sacrificed initiative and growth for limitation and for physical safety.

When will we learn that we do not solve problems by running away from them, nor difficult situations by refusing to face them. God did not put us into this world to be cowards, but to be victors. He did not put us here to be crushed by life, but to conquer it. He did not put us here to be paupers, but to be kings.

Maybe you are wondering what all this has to do with you and just how the self-centeredness and introversion of medieval monks have any bearing upon your life and the dilemmas which you face. Well, just this: There are other runaways besides those who seek sanctuary in monastic life. We refer to the great army of people who seek security in small things, who evade responsibility, who refuse to face life because it is difficult, who are satisfied with less than their best, who refuse to confront their problems, who follow the line of least resistance. And that vast host of cramped minds always seeking the safety and protection of an institution, job or position because of guaranteed incomes at a small expenditure of effort. "If I do my part," they say, "I will always be taken care of."

We are forever trying to dodge problems that are difficult. We are forever trying to run away from the things that are uncongenial and unpleasant. Instead of letting our light shine we hide it under a basket. We are like the impractical poet who said, "Oh that I had the wings of a dove, then I would fly away and be at rest." Rest does not come from evading problems, but by facing them. He who runs away will have to fight another day. The reason we cannot run away from our problems is because we cannot run away from ourselves. The problem and the self are but two ends of the same thing. They are like a man and his shadow. Where the self goes the problem goes. And the self always catches up with the man who tries to run away from it.

"Military authorities tell us that the bravest soldiers are not those who are wholly without fear, and not those who recklessly and foolishly expose themselves to the shot and shell of the enemy. They say the bravest men are those who, in spite of fear and in full knowledge of danger, face all the enemy can give and press on to victory. So it is in life. They live best

who face life's realities, and press on to ulti-
mate victory."

THE THINGS THAT NEED ALTERING

The prodigal son was seeking a new environment but what he really needed was a new
attitude toward life. The way out of difficult
circumstances is not by a change of location,
but by a change of mind. The things that need
altering are not the unfavorable conditions in
the outer world, but the consciousness within.
The things that need changing are not the persons and difficulties we meet, but our attitude
toward them and our thoughts about them.
To alter life we must go to its roots. We must
painstakingly check every thought and belief
before it becomes a part of consciousness.

Ask yourself: Is this thought God-like? Does
it have the quality of Jesus' thinking? Is it a
positive or constructive thought? Is it life giving? Is it affirmative? If the answer is No, then
go to work on it. Do something about it. Raise
your mind to God and repudiate everything
that is untrue, unlike God.

Probably the greatest problem in spiritual
therapeutics is the problem of self-centered-

ness. The self-centered man is not only an un-happy man but a sick man. He is the pulse-feeler, the temperature-taker and the symptom-tabulator. He always is circumscribed by his absorption in the immediate. He is held in bondage by morbid introspection, routine think-ing and too much attention to workings of his own mind. He is enslaved by his own mental moods and fluctuations. He is the victim of all those negative qualities so vigorously de-nounced by the Master. Jesus had no sympathy with little thoughts or little minds, but held that we should at all times be bigger than our-selves and greater than the circumstances in our lives.

"The ancients used to tell their children of Narcissus, the beautiful youth who paused in the chase to drink from a pool whose waters were crystal clear. For the first time he saw his face. He had never been permitted to see his image because a prophet had warned his mother that he would live to manhood only if he never gazed upon himself. When he looked into the water he saw that he was beautiful and so enamored was he of his own image that he lay down upon the grass to gaze at his re-flection. There he lay until he began to pine away. Neither Apollo's golden chariot which came rolling over the hills in the morning nor Diana's silver car which coursed through the star-lit streets by night could attract his attention from his own beautiful face. There he stayed, growing thinner and thinner until he died."

Such, thought the ancients, is the sad destiny of any one who grows self-centered. The self-centered mind is a closed mind which leads to spiritual death.

The parable of the prodigal son is in reality what the psychologist would call the case histories of two self-centered men, the one who went away—turned his ego-centricity outward, and the other who stayed at home—turned his ego-centricity inward. Both had "me" at the center and both were impoverished by the self. The younger son took his first step away from God when he said, "Give ME the portion of goods that falleth to me," and the older son when he said, "Thou never gavest ME" a kid that I might make merry with MY friends.

How then shall we bring this particular run-away back home? How shall we break the captivity of his hedged-in soul? How shall we liberate him from his self imposed prison?

There is only one way, as Isaiah said, "Look unto me and be ye saved, all the ends of the earth." In other words, look away from self to God. "Be absent from the body and present with the Lord."

If you would find God, then you must lose self. If you would be emancipated from the untoward settings in your life, then you must dedicate yourself to the high purposes of God's Kingdom. If you would let go of your ailments, then you must let go of self. You must not try to drive them out by will power or personal effort, but by properly impressing the subconscious to let go. "Look unto me" means to consecrate yourself to a lofty and enduring Cause, to something bigger than yourself.

When Jesus began his earthly ministry He found men seeking divine help through obedience to laws, rituals and rules. He knew that they were getting nowhere because it all ended in self righteousness. Their conformity to all the laws was cold and calculating. The legalists of His day had so embellished the Mosaic law with meaningless subtleties that none but a trained mind could understand it. "They had two hundred and forty-eight affirmative precepts, in keeping with the number of members in the human body, and three hundred and sixty-five negative precepts, in keeping with as many days in the year and the number of arteries and veins of the human body, the total of which (six hundred and thirteen) was the exact number of letters in the Decalogue."

Their worship was perfunctory and theatrical. Their religious desire was to be seen and approved of men. Their religion only narrowed their lives and intensified their selfishness. It robbed them of the freedom and happiness which only the detached self can know. Instead of adding power to their lives, it made them soft and weak. Instead of a force, it was a form. Jesus called them to find the Larger Man within. He called them to self denial, surrender and detachment as the true way of salvation.

To the young lawyer who approached Jesus with the question, "Master, which is the great commandment in the law?" He quickly quoted (Deut. 6; 4, 5): "Hear, O Israel: The Lord our God is one Lord; And thou shalt love the Lord thy God with all thine heart, and with all thy soul, and with all thy might." Then, as if to strengthen the teaching of Moses, He added quickly: "Thou shalt love thy neighbor as thyself." Why do you suppose He added the last line? It was to set forth the true nature of the Christian religion, which is the two-fold love of God and man. He was calling them to self-dedication, to a Cause that was bigger than themselves. First, a supreme love towards God and, second, a love toward their fellow men which was equal to their love for themselves.

The difference between static religion and dynamic religion is love, and where Love is there is no lack. Thus the Christian religion is really love in action. "On these two commandments hang all the law and the prophets." When a man is perfectly balanced between these two great love commandments, he may be said to be in Heaven, for "Love always has met and always will meet every human need."

LOOKING BACK

But there is another runaway which is very common among the soldiers of the cross and that is the man who looks back. "No man having put his hand to the plow, and (is) looking back," said Jesus, "is fit for the Kingdom of Heaven." Jesus did not want people to rush into His Kingdom blindly. He wanted them to be sure of themselves, to be sure of the cost before making a decision. Enlistment in the Kingdom of God was a serious step and it added great responsibilities. Once a man had set his face toward Truth, there could be no turning back without serious consequences, without losing all the momentum which he had gained in his previous endeavor. To Him it was a life enlistment, a life commitment, and any one who deserted would find himself worse off than before.

As the Bible says, "The last state of that man is worse than the first." That is why Jesus counseled candidates for His Kingdom to consider fully what they were about to do before they took the step.

The Truth is not something that can be picked up and laid down at will, nor can it be deserted successfully when once begun. The Kingdom of Heaven is like the yeast in the lump of dough. When once recognized (set in motion), it must be allowed to germinate until it permeates the whole mass. If the Truth is to make us free then it must be allowed to fill the whole consciousness. Once begun it must be forever. There can be no interference and no foreshortening of the process without disastrous results.

Just as a strong man's muscles begin to atrophy and go into disease when he stops exercising, so the inactive Truth student begins to disintegrate and lower the tone of his life when he gives up the practice of Truth. He opens himself and his circumstances to disaster and disharmony, lets down his health and weakens and undermines the character. The unfinished task becomes an obstacle in his life. The forces set in motion for Good are now turned into disease and other forms of ill.

Discipleship is not won by spasmodic effort but by consecration and self-dedication. In the ninth chapter of St. Luke's Gospel is the story of three men who wanted to become disciples but who were not fully conscious of what enlistment entailed. Consequently Jesus told them to think it over and to consider fully what they contemplated doing before giving a final answer.

The first man came saying, "I will follow thee." But Jesus saw that this man was looking for personal gain and promptly discouraged him by pointing out the sacrifices he would have to make. It was not an encouraging picture that Jesus painted but it had the desired effect. "Foxes have holes, and the birds of the

air have nests; but the Son of Man hath not
where to lay his head."

When Jesus addressed the second man asking if he were ready to follow Him, the man
answered, "Lord, suffer me first to go and bury
my father." This man's father was not dead;
he was old and feeble, needing care, and the
son felt he should go home and look after him
until death. Then he would come and follow
Jesus. And why not; after all, he considered
there was no hurry about the matter, and it
would be much easier to enter upon his new
work when the old responsibilities were off his
mind. This candidate obviously was procrasti-
nating, and Jesus told him that the Kingdom
required haste and could not await his convenience. It must take precedence over everything else in a man's life. "Let the dead bury
their dead; but go thou and preach the Kingdom of God."

The third man was divided in his thought.
He wanted to eat his cake and have it too. "I
will follow Thee," he said, "but let me first go
bid them farewell, which are at home in my
house." This man wanted to follow Jesus but
he also wanted to be at home with his people.
His dedication was half-hearted because his

mind was divided. He was not consecrated to the work ahead. He was trying to live in two places at the same time—trying to think in two directions. Jesus saw all this and that is why He told him that "No man, having put his hand to the plow and (is) looking back, is fit for the Kingdom of Heaven."

It once was suggested by A. J. Gossip that should a man stroll into a recruiting station offering to give fifteen minutes each morning and evening to the army, provided, of course, that he was not too busy, he probably would be turned away with an oath. "We are at war, and your wretched business is of no importance. The army claims not something you think you can spare, but you. All that you have, all that you are and all that you hope to be. If you are not willing to give us that, then out of this." How often we seek to settle cheaply with God. But He is not satisfied with part of the heart, part of the soul and part of the mind. The Lord asks the whole man. It must be a wholehearted dedication. It must be all out devotion to His Kingdom.

It is interesting to note that in dealing with the third man Jesus used the illustration of a Syrian farmer. "He had his hand to the plow because in the East the plow had only one handle." Here was a farmer trying to plow with a divided mind. He was trying to think in two directions at the same time. He was trying to go forward by thinking backward. Like the man who wanted to be with Jesus and with his own people at the same time, he was torn between two loyalties. He could not make up his mind.

"God's causes," says George Adam Smith, "are never destroyed by being blown up, but by being sat upon." Yes, the urgent note of decision has often been left out. Jesus told this man that he must be one thing or the other— do one thing or the other. His self surrender must be complete. To plow a straight furrow he must look straight ahead. He must fix his eye upon some object ahead of him and go straight to it. You must do the same thing in life. You must plow straight toward God or toward self.

DECIDE

The trouble with too many people is that they pray the prayer of St. Augustine: "Oh God, make me pure, but not just now." The vacillating attitude in Truth is just as devastating as the ills from which we suffer. "Irresolution is a worse vice than rashness. He that shoots best may sometimes hit the mark; but he that shoots not at all can never hit it." Indecision is one of man's worst enemies. It is a disease of the will and creates a disproportion between the practical and spiritual faculties of the mind. The vacillating man, however efficient and strong in other matters, is always by-passed by the man who knows what he wants to do and does it.

Joshua said, "Choose ye this day whom ye will serve." Before you can accomplish anything in spiritual work you first must make your decision. When you go to a hardware store you must decide whether you want a lawn mower or a hose; at a soda fountain, whether you will have a malted milk or a banana split. It is not enough for a suitor to tell his bride-to-be that he loves her as much as other girls. "Love demands the undivided heart." A man who does not know whether he wants to be a doctor or a lawyer is liable to fail at both. No man can follow two ideas and get one result. "No great deed is done by falterers who ask for certainty."

The difference between accomplishment and

failure, between weakness and power, between mediocrity and excellence is DECISION. The difference between answered and unaswered prayer is the difference between faith in God and faith in your problem. Thus you must decide in the beginning of a prayer which has the greater power, your problem or God.

There is a cure for indecision and it is found in St. Paul's epistle to the Philippians, "This one thing I do, forgetting those things which are behind, and reaching forth to those things which are before, I press toward the mark." "I am going to trust God, and nothing else." Would you have an educated will? Then you must have a definite goal. You must be one-pointed in vision. You must be self-reliant, self-restrained, self-directed and self-controlled.

The regenerated life always begins with a change of mind and a wholly dedicated self. Indeed, these are the central claims of Jesus: "He that loveth father or mother more than me is not worthy of me." "No man, having put his hand to the plow, and looking back, is fit for the Kingdom of God." "He that loseth his life for my sake shall find it." "Sell that which thou hast . . . and come follow me." The first requirement of discipleship is willingness to leave everything else; to cut yourself off from all preconceived ideas. But change is so dangerous, you say: There always is the possibility that I may "throw the baby out with the bath," or the spoon with the salad. That is true, but the one thing more dangerous than change is failure to change.

We must grow toward God or perish. It doesn't make any difference how many demonstrations you may have had in the past. The question is, how many are you having now. Are you growing; are you growing in understanding, in faith, in power, in consciousness? If your answer to these questions is no, if all your achievements lie behind you, then you have stopped growing, and you are stagnating in spiritual death.

BLESSED IS THE MAN
WHO KEEPS GROWING

Jesus said: "Blessed is the man who hungers and thirsts after righteousness." Blessed is the man who never is satisfied. Blessed is the man who keeps growing, for only he shall be filled. Blessed is the man who keeps on keeping on. Blessed is the man who does not know when he is beaten. Blessed is the man who does not know how to compromise. Blessed is the man who does not know when to stop praying. Blessed is the man who never gives up. As Louis Untermeyer says in his poem on prayer:

"From compromise and things half done
    Keep me with stern and stubborn pride.
And when, at last, the fight is won,
    God, keep me still unsatisfied."

The basic cause of most failures in life is the fact that most people do not go far enough. They do not hold on long enough. They work for things instead of working to bring their consciousness up to the highest point of efficiency; in other words, they stop short of success. They lack continuity and persistency. They want results but they lack the staying power necessary to get them.

What do we mean by "staying power?" We mean the ability to hold on even when the facts contradict the results we are after. We mean the tenacity of purpose which holds a vision so tightly that nothing can separate us from it. If we have persistency then obstacles and difficulties will bend to our will. If we do not have it then we must cultivate it. "Await the issue," said Carlyle. "In all battles if we await the issue, each fighter prospers according to his right. His right and his might, at the close of the account, were one and the same."

The victorious man always is the persistent man. Confusion cannot frustrate him, drudgery cannot weary him, defeats cannot discourage him, difficulties cannot fret him, disappointments cannot deter him. No matter what happens, he will persist for persistence is part of his nature. The dictionary defines persistency as the ability "to continue steadfastly in a course of conduct against opposing motives." To the chemist it is experiment after experiment. To the mathematician it is problem after problem. To the lawyer it is trial after trial. To the student it is book after book. To the musician it is lesson after lesson. To the Christian it is prayer after prayer. To the minister it is sermon after sermon. To the strong man it is exercise after exercise. To the soldier it is battle after battle. Efficiency comes out of persistency.

FAITH IN YOUR GOAL

When Jesus said the Kingdom of God is within you, He meant that you are packed with invisible potentialities. Thus what comes out of your Kingdom will come in response to your call. You should not make the mistake therefore of thinking that you cannot accomplish what you set out to do simply because you do not see the way clearly. The very intensity of your faith is guarantee of its fulfillment. You do not need to see the end of the road. All you need is light for the next step. Faith in your goal and persistent effort will do the rest. There is no doubt about it.

If you do your part God will do His part. It is just as simple as making a kodak picture from a negative under the light. If you send out your wishes and desires with the same confidence that you place the sensitized paper and negative under a light, they will attract their affinities and soon take shape as tangible things. God's part is to develop the film and your part is to develop the picture and bring it forth.

The trouble with most people who do not get results from their prayers is lack of coordination between their mind pictures (desires) and actual results. They do not understand the relation of thought to accomplishment. They start out with great enthusiasm but setbacks come and their visions are soon dimmed. Their grip on their mind-pictures was not strong enough. They did not understand the mighty power of a focussed mind to bring their visions into actual form. "If thine eye be single," says the Bible, "thy whole body shall be full of light."

Now ask yourself how much of a grip your vision has on you. Does it hold you; do you hold it with such a force that nothing in the world can separate you from it, or do you hold it so lightly that the least thing throws you off the track and discourages you from trying to make it real?

"Where there is no vision," says the book of Proverbs, "the people perish." Don't you see that there is a very definite relation between your visions and your life, and that if you have no visions, no dreams, and no ideals you are merely stagnating and dying in your tracks? Wouldn't it be better therefore to uncover the things which are diverting you from your aims and put them to flight? It certainly would, and there is no better time to start than right now.

Then how will you begin? By systematically putting out of your mind forever any thought that anybody, or anything, or any combination of things, can ever deter you or prevent you from reaching your goal. Let come what may, fire, flood or riot—criticism, opposition or disappointment—starvation, discouragement or misfortune of any kind, nothing in all the world can possibly divert you from your course. No matter how dark and threatening the appearance may be, you will keep working, keep visualizing your dream until God opens it for fulfillment. This is the attitude that will draw your own to you.

The promise is that you "shall reap if you faint not." If you have the tenacity and grit to hold on to the finish, if you refuse to recognize defeat, then you will get what you want.

What, then, shall we say to the potential runaways and how shall we convince them of the error of their ways? By showing them that their problems are not in their environment, as they are so prone to believe, but in their minds, and that what is in their minds will follow them wherever they go—if they fail to meet a problem in one place they will have to face it in some other place. The thing the deserter needs to learn is that he is not dealing with persons, circumstances, conditions and things, but with his thoughts about persons, circumstances, conditions and things.

It is thought that determines every movement of a man's life—whether he goes up or down. It is wrong thought that takes him away from God and right thought that brings him back.

When the children of Israel thought toward Egypt they marched toward Egypt; when they thought toward Canaan they marched toward Canaan. When a man thinks toward God he moves toward the better and greater things of life; when he thinks toward self (away from God) he moves toward limitation, retrogression and loss. It is not God Who sends us into pig pens to feed with the swine, but our thought of self. When we are absent from the Father's House, the Good is absent too; and the absence of the Good means suffering, limitation and want.

ONE MIND

In the Parable of the Prodigal Son, Jesus made it clear that we are surrounded by a mental principle which he designated as the Father's House, or Universal Mind, which receives the impress of our thought and acts upon it creatively and intelligently. We think into It and It gives back to us the results of our thinking. It acts upon our thought exactly as we think it. It responds to us by corresponding precisely to our states of mind. This Mind knows us by that which we know about ourselves; It accepts only that which we believe. Being subjective to our thought, It cannot know anything else; it always accepts and reflects us as we are. It always does for us only what we believe It can do; It always gives to us only what we believe It can give.

There is no such thing as your mind, my mind, some one else's mind, and God's Mind. There is, as St. Paul pointed out, just One Mind, in Whom we live, move and have our being, and which makes things and conditions out of ideas. When we understand this, that "THOUGHTS ARE THINGS AND THINGS ARE IDEAS," and that "THERE IS NOTHING OUT OF WHICH WE MAKE THINGS EXCEPT IDEAS," then we shall approach all problems, troubles and difficulties by resolving them into right thoughts. We shall overcome them by changing our thought about them.

As Plotinus said, "I do not argue; I contemplate; and as I contemplate I let fall the forms of my thought." This is the way nature creates. It contemplates through its conscious mind. As a result of its contemplation it lets fall the seeds of its thought into the Universal Subjective, which, being Law, produces the thing thought of. Now we must expect to find, and do find the same thing reenacted in man. "This means that whatever man thinks (whether it be what he calls good or bad) falls into this Universal Creative Medium, is accepted by It, is at once acted upon, begins to take form, and unless neutralized tends to become a thing in the objective world." (Science of Mind.)

The next thing we note about the Divine Creative Principle is that It already has provided more than we shall ever need. What we call limitation is nothing more than our own limited thought. There can be no such thing as limitation itself. There is nothing to limit us but our ignorance. Ignorance is our worst enemy, because it creates separation, limitation, sickness, inferiority, blundering and failure. There is no power in the Universe that tries or tempts us; there is no power that withholds from us but our own thought. "Son, thou art ever with me and all that I have is thine."

The Universe gives to all men liberally, but we tune into Its givingness or tune out of It according to the polarity of our thought.

The law that separates us unifies us. The law that takes away is the law that gives. The law that makes us slaves is the law that makes us free. The law that makes us sick is the law that makes us well. The law that makes us poor is the law that makes us rich. There is just one law and the way we use it. We specialize it through our thought and subjective tendencies. It responds to us by corresponding to our states of mind. It works according to our belief. It moves according to our consciousness. It gives according to our acceptance.

As Ernest Holmes says, "There is One Infinite Mind from which all things come; this Mind is through, in and around man. It is the only Mind there is, and every time man thinks he uses It. There is One Infinite Spirit, and every time man says " 'I AM' " he proclaims It. There is One Infinite Substance, and every time man moves he moves in It. There is One Infinite Law, and every time man thinks he sets it in motion. There is One Infinite God, and every time man speaks to this God he receives a direct answer. One! One! One! 'I am God and beside me there is none else.' There is One Limitless Life, which returns to the thinker what he thinks into It. One! One! One! 'In all, over all, through all.' "

With this knowledge it is easy to see why man automatically attracts to himself what he is, and why, if he does not like the things he is attracting, he can change them by changing his thought and the polarity of his faith. The mental switch governing the distribution of God's gifts is a two-way switch very similar to the light switches in our homes. When the switch is turned in the upward position, the light comes in and floods the room. When it is turned in the downward position, the light goes off and darkness prevails. Light and darkness are but two ends of the same thing—the presence and the absence of light, and the switch merely tunes into one or the other according to the direction in which it faces, just as the polarity of our thought tunes into feast or famine in accord with the direction in which it faces.

If our mind is in the ascendancy (lifted up to God) and harmonized with Divine thought, then it will strengthen our life and bring the power and gifts of God into expression. If it is in the descending scale, then it will undermine our life and bring darkness, weakness, disharmony and disaster into expression.

TURN TO THE CHART

If you would like to see how this law works, turn now to the chart at the front of the book and there note some of the things which take you out of the Father's House and into the "far country" of limitation and want. When you know the nature of things that take you out of His Presence (separate you from your good), then you can, by carefully avoiding them, learn how to keep yourself in His Presence. The real problem in living is not motion, but direction. Religion is not an opiate for feeble minds. It is a rule of life. Those who live by the rule live in a better world than those who do not. Mouthing creeds, burning candles and singing hymns are meaningless if they are not integrated with life.

Now, as you study the chart you will notice, first, that the Life out of which all things are made, flowing from the Father's House (Infinite Source of Supply), is neither good nor evil, neither positive nor negative, neither constructive nor destructive. It is just Life

Energy—pure, uncontaminated and free. In its primary (Original) state as it comes from God and unrelated to man's thought, It expresses Perfection, Wholeness, Power and every form of Good. In its secondary, or used state, that is when it has been put through man's thought, It expresses whatever the tendency of man's mind and the molds of his thought have made for it. Working only through thought, imagination and will, It pours Itself into any mold or matrix that is provided for it.

The energy that is turned into discord, sickness, failure, unhappiness, sorrow and other negative forms in no way differs from the energy that expresses itself in the forms of peace, health, success, happiness and joy. The difference is not in the life of energy, but in the thought that directs it into constructive or destructive channels. If the thought is in the ascending scale, then it will produce perfection, wholeness and every form of Good. If it is in the descending scale, then it will produce just the reverse of these—it will open itself to every form of evil.

"Behold my face for evermore." "Look unto me, and be ye saved, all the ends of the earth." In other words, Look up and not down; think

up and not down. Since it always is consciousness that determines what the outcome of any
situation will be, it is useless to treat problems,
conditions or things.

The business of practical religion is not so
much to relieve a man of his physical distresses
and financial limitations, as to build a consciousness without disease, without limitation
and without panic. It involves setting up a new
order of thinking and a new rule of life. Its
goal is the establishment of a new way of living,
in which negative and destructive thoughts and
feelings shall never get a foothold; in which
life shall be measured not by what happens in
the world but by what happens in man. Reason
as we will, our lives and our experiences are
the result of our thinking, and both "are
peopled with the personifications of our
thoughts and ideas."

Nothing is real to us unless we make it real.
Nothing can touch us unless we let it touch
us. Imperfection in any form is an effect, and
back of the effect is an idea which is the cause
of the effect. Divine Energy flowing from the
Infinite Source is perfect, but man, through his
negative thinking, causes it to appear to be
imperfect. Through uplifted thought "he is able

to uncover the appearance of imperfection and reveal the Perfect Idea."

BELIEF IN SEPARATION

We can only speculate as to why the younger son left his Father's House to go into the "far country." It could have been any one of a hundred things familiar to us all. It could have been inharmony, selfishness, misery, quarreling, jealousy, envy, bitterness, hatred, disagreement, dissatisfaction, disappointment, or any one of the countless annoying and harassing experiences which beset man's path. We could name scores of such possible reasons and we could sum them up in the words "belief in separation." The younger son had turned his stream of consciousness from God to the world, and the result was starvation. His real sin was not in his desire for something better, but in his belief in separation. When he ceased to identify himself with God—the Whole, he began to be in want. There was separation in his soul, and separation in the soul means separation in the world.

Jesus said: "The Kingdom of God is within you" (within your consciousness), and all success in prayer is dependent upon the realization and embodiment of this idea, and in our ability to abide (live) in it. One Mind, in whom we all live, move and have our being; upon which we shall depend, and upon Whom we shall draw for everything we need. God and man are inseparable as Spirit and identity; and it is impossible for them to be separated— except in belief.

"The answer to every question is within man, because man is within Spirit, and Spirit is an indivisible whole. The solution to every problem is within man; the healing of all disease is within man; the forgiveness of sin is within man." Heaven is within man: That is why Jesus said, "I and the Father are One," and "The Kingdom of God is Within you." He knew that since every apparent problem was due to a belief in a separate selfhood it could be healed only if the self were re-united with God, the Whole.

But how does the reunion take place, and how, if we already live, move and have our being in God, can we do anything to bring Him any closer to us? What more can we do to place ourselves and our affairs in His hands? Well, the truth is that there is nothing we can do to bring God **any** closer to us. The real problem in the "far country" is not to bring God any closer to us, but to bring ourselves closer to God. God is our being and our life. We are in His Spirit now but we do not know it; and, as Jesus said, we must know the Truth before It can make us free. To raise our thoughts to God is to place ourselves in His hands, and to consciously enter His Presence, so that we may feel His Life and Power in every atom of our being.

God works according to our needs only when our thoughts and desires are adjusted to His Mind and Will. The Spirit then comes in and does whatever we wish to have done. There is no struggle or strain on our part, but just a quiet confidence and willingness to let the Spirit take possession of us and make us every whit whole. When our thoughts are up, God will do for us whatever we wish Him to do, providing, and this is the important point, that we do not neutralize our good by an opposite thought, or by a contrary belief.

LOVINGLY IN THE HANDS OF THE FATHER

Thousands of persons in the last ten years have found magic performance in the right use of Evelyn Whittell's affirmation, "Lovingly in the hands of the Father." By lifting their thoughts to God, and by repeating these words every time a need came to their minds, they have overcome seemingly insurmountable problems, and demonstrated money, positions, health and untold good. "I place myself and all my affairs lovingly in the hands of the Father, with a childlike trust. That which is for my highest good shall come to me."

Actually there is no special magic or particular charm in this particular affirmation, but like any other well chosen words, rightly used with detachment and spiritual relaxation, it will bring marvelous results. The statement by and of itself is really nothing more than a vehicle, so to speak, by which to shift our problem and responsibility for its solution from our shoulders to God's. It must be backed up with the deep conviction and faith that what we involve in the statement is true. When we speak the words, we must believe that what we desire to have done is being done now, and that it is being done by a Power that is able to do all things. We must believe it so firmly that we no longer take anxious thought about it.

When we place ourselves and our affairs

"lovingly in the hands of the Father," we must be willing to leave them there and to know that the Spirit will do that which is best for us. Since God is able to give us and to do for us much more than we ask or even think, it must be His Will and not ours. The formula (any formula) will work for that which we want when we keep the thought of lack out of our minds—and it cannot work in any other way.

The thing that most people do not seem to understand, however, is that there is a vast difference between belief in God and the Consciousness of His Presence. Unfortunately for the vast number of Christians, they depend upon their belief in God to get them through the tight places of life when it really is the Consciousness of His Presence that does the work. Belief without realization is like faith without works. It is dead.

St. Paul said: "Let this Mind be in you, which was also in Christ Jesus." Let it. Do you hear? Let it be in you, not outside you. Let it be active in your mind and consciousness. Let it be active in your life and affairs. Do you see the difference between belief in God and the Consciousness of His Presence? It is the difference between "O God" and "My God." It is the difference between static power and dynamic power, between hoping and having. It is the difference between unanswered and answered prayer. It is the difference between begging and accepting.

To depend solely upon your belief in God to fulfill your needs is like depending upon the water in the reservoir to carry itself into your home. Unless you have a connection with the water main, there will be no water in your pipes. To "Let this Mind be in you" means to pass from belief to realization. To be conscious of God's Presence, is to be in His Presence and to have all your needs supplied automatically.

But how does one pass from belief to realization? How does one let this Mind be in him which daily resurrects, vitalizes, renews and re-creates the Divine Image? There are two ways in which this may be achieved: First, by keeping the mind elevated to God, and, second, by constantly guarding our thoughts against negatives, against worry, fear, uncertainty, anxiety, doubt and evil until we are able to maintain a perfect balance between wear and tear, and to keep ourselves on the constructive and affirmative side of Good.

Most Christians accept God in their heads, and that is only half the process. The other half is to realize His Presence in the depths of their minds. Indeed, God has little chance with any man until that man is conscious of His Presence. If we would contact Him vitally in practice, then we must have the conscious, loving recognition of His Presence in every last detail of our lives. We must pass from "O God" to "My God"—from belief to realization. It is the difference between talking and having, between seeing and possessing. Our watchword must be: Immanuel—God with us.

"Think of self, Trouble grows;

Think of God, Trouble goes."

But let us again think of some of those things which take us out of God's hands and turn off the current so that we cease to be instruments of His Power. What are these things? They are all the negative thoughts, reactions and attitudes which make us inferior and keep us from our good. It is not God Who punishes us when we leave His House; we punish ourselves by going away from the place where good things are to be found. When we are away, "the good is absent; and the absence of good means evil, the entering into of which means punishment."

Just as positive and constructive trends of mind keep up in the Father's House, so negative and destructive trends take us out of it.

Jesus said: "He that gathereth not with me scattereth." Just as the positive (true) thought unites the mind so the negative (wrong) thought divides it. Our worthiness to be called sons therefore is determined not by any outer act or profession, but by keeping our minds off self and on God, and by keeping our wills under His control. It is the difference between seeing life through a divided mind from the lower level of the personal self and seeing it through the united mind from the higher level of the Divine Self.

We never are deprived of anything good and never separated from God's blessings so long as we face Home, so long as we keep our thoughts up to the One Source from which everything comes and so long as we know that nothing in the Universe opposes our Good. That is the high meaning of facing Home. So long as we think of ourselves as separated from God because of our waywardness, our sin, insobriety, disobedience and immorality, our prayers are ineffectual and unproductive. God's goodness does not turn upon human weakness nor the forces that play upon the lower self, but upon the trend of man's thought and the polarity of his faith.

GOD DOES NOT KNOW EVIL

The Spirit of God does not know evil and makes no distinction between a sinning man and a good man. "God does not know both good and evil." "There is no sin but a mistake, and no punishment but an inevitable consequence." Wrong doing is punished for the same reason that right doing is rewarded. Both results come from going with or against the law of cause and effect, which always is at work. The Law is sure and certain. So long as a man makes mistakes so long will he continue to be hurt by the Law. What then is the solution of the problem of evil? To stop living and thinking in the lower brackets, of the personal self. Destructive habits disappear when we cease to indulge them and when we stop misusing the law of freedom.

The promise is that "If thou return to the Almighty, thou shalt be built up." When we return our whole being to God and live daily in His presence, evil habits will lose their power over us and the problem of evil will be solved automatically. "I will forgive their iniquity, and I will remember their sin no more."

In the Father's House there is no place for inferiority, disagreement, temper, unhappiness, remorse or regrets. There is no place for disappointment and there is no past. There is only one here and now, and that is eternal. In the story of the ploughman, Jesus points out that the man who turns away from, or looks back upon his home, is not fit for the Kingdom of Heaven and therefore cannot live in it. Every backward look, every depressed thought, every sorrow, every regret, every negative emotion and every un-Christlike attitude is a detour, a serious delay on the pathway of Truth.

When Jesus said to the elder brother, "Son, thou art ever with me, and all that I have is thine," He meant that to be in-Christed, or continually supplied with good things from on High, we must keep our minds at home and our thoughts under control. Then "we shall discover that we are Self-sustained, Self-maintained and Self-governed, and that we have no responsibility for anything but the thought that is in our minds."

The door that opens into the Father's House is narrow because it admits only the Real Self

—the son. You cannot be a dual self and at the same time live in the Father's House. You cannot have two minds—one human and one divine. You can have only the mind of Christ. There is room only for the Real Self. Neither can you lean on outside forces, persons or "pull." In the Household of God you must live your own life with God and allow all others to do the same.

To live with God is not only to live with the best but to have the best. So long as you keep your thoughts on God you will be in His House. So long as you desire the good you will receive the good. But when you begin to desire what is not good you leave His House. Then you automatically cut yourself off from the essentials of life and enter into a great void of emptiness, limitation and loss.

Isaiah says: "They that wait upon the Lord shall renew their strength; they shall mount up with wings as eagles; they shall run, and not be weary; they shall walk, and not faint." This means that when your whole mind is centered in God then your whole world will improve. "Behold, I make all things new." The Creative Power will set to work at once to recreate, rebuild and harmonize everything in your body and affairs. Your health will improve. Your finances will become better. Your environment will be more congenial. You will attract greater opportunities, more agreeable people and circumstances will lose their power over you. In other words, you will have reversed the whole process and direction of your life. Instead of seeking opportunities and things as in other days, opportunities and things will seek you.

You are now victory-organized and everything you do will be a success because you are in the Father's House. "Thanks be to God, Who giveth us the victory through our Lord Jesus Christ." Does that mean that you will have no more unpleasant experiences? Not at all, but that you will be in a better and more favorable position to master them. In the Father's House you will not be disturbed by them, because Heaven is on your side and all the power of God is working in your behalf.

So you see nothing is ever gained by running away from the Father's House, but everything is gained by remaining at home—keeping a true and balanced relation to God. God did not save Jesus from the cross. He did not prevent Daniel from falling into the lions' den, nor the

Hebrew young men from falling into the fiery furnace; but if we are conscious of His Presence He will always shut the mouths of the lions and bring us safely through every untoward experience unharmed and unscathed.

Jesus did not take His disciples out of the world, but He taught them how to live masterfully and successfully in the world. He said, "Work out your own salvation," not by a pious and passive belief in God but by proving your own divinity for yourself, by perceiving that God (the Good) and your consciousness are one, and by discovering that there is no power but the power of your own Christ mind, and that this power is God.

It never made any difference to Jesus how trying or how extenuating the circumstances were, He never made any compromise with evil nor looked outside of nor away from His Consciousness for anything. "He proved His Principle to be one, and included himself in the Whole, therefore He had nothing to get rid of but everything to praise and glorify." Heaven is not won by contingencies, disasters, failures and disappointments, but by overcoming them. Since nothing but a belief can ever really separate us from the Love of God, we are never burdened with more than we can bear. It may seem at times as though we are terribly incompetent and inadequate to meet the problems that crowd our lives, but that is so only when we view these problems from a divided mind and from the lower level of the human or personal self.

Father and Son is not just a beautiful theory but a life to be lived. Praying without ceasing means keeping the thoughts continually up to God. It is the only way we shall ever overcome the evil and cause all things to work together for good.

EQUANIMITY

Some one has said that the greatest word in any language is "Equanimity," which as the dictionary says means: "Evenness of mind or temper; composure of spirit: especially calmness and steadiness amid trying circumstances; as to bear losses with equanimity." Now ask yourself if you meet the test of equanimity. Ask yourself if you are calm and collected under all circumstances.

When trouble comes, do you rise above it as master or do you buckle under it as a slave? When personal problems come into your life, do you demagnetize them by impersonalizing them and giving them to God, or do you magnify them by dwelling upon them and holding them tightly in your thought? In a sudden crisis or emergency, do you keep peaceful and serene, or do you become frightened, panic stricken and confused? When people criticize, slander and malign you, do you become angry or frustrated, or do you make yourself bigger than calumny and your opponent by refusing to allow them to touch you? Are you the victim of worry, anxiety, doubt and fear? Are you at the mercy of some inferiority complex which easily defeats and discourages you?

If your answer to any of these questions is yes, then you are out of adjustment with God and you lack equanimity. You are, so to speak, living without God and you are subdued by the very things you were meant to subdue.

The difficulty with most people is that they have not learned how to live successfully in trouble—by living outside it. They have not learned how to rise above distractions and dilemmas by changing their thoughts and attitudes toward them. If a loved one is taken ill, or a promise is broken, or reverses come, they are then completely off balance and are unable for the time being to carry on their work. They are crippled and handicapped, not because of their troubles but because they have not learned how to live successfully and triumphantly with them. Instead of conquering them, they are conquered by them. They dream of panic-proof, sound-proof shelters where they imagine trouble can never reach them, where there is no tension and WHERE the water is never muddied. But there is no such security apart from the "peace of God, which passeth all understanding."

THE WAY TO CONQUER DIFFICULTIES

The way to conquer difficulties is not by fighting nor running away from them, but by living with a triumphant faith. The towering and successful life does not mean one free from emergencies, crises, disappointments, frustrations and delays, but one who lives with "an unfaltering faith in an unfailing God." The victorious life is the tranquil life, rooted in God and more than equal to any need. The God-centered man does not moan and groan, shudder and collapse when big problems and great obstacles confront him. He knows at all times and under all circumstances that there is a power within him greater than anything in the world. He has found in the depths of his being a divine, stabilizing power which carries him triumphantly through every storm that blows.

Living with the peace of God in his heart man is not only lifted above his troubles but is unaffected by them. They are solved for him by a Power not his own.

The real task of practical religion is not to make a man pious, but to validate the proven principles of Jesus and to make them operative in his life. It is not enough to worship Jesus. It is not enough to be a church member. It is not enough to be a Truth student. It is not enough to have God in our heads. The thing that really counts and gives man power over his world is to live with an intimate sense of God's Presence in his daily life.

If you are overwhelmed with problems, you will find it helpful, in addition to the other instruction in this book, to arise half an hour earlier every morning and read, meditatively, the fifteenth chapter of St. John, the sixth chapter of St. Matthew, the fifty-fifth chapter of

Isaiah, and the twenty-third, the thirty-seventh, the ninetieth and the ninety-first Psalms. It is one of the quickest ways to get the power to face your life as it is.

What made Jesus' life so great was not the phenomenal things that He did but the power by which He lived; not His achievements but the quality of His soul. He did not boast of physical or mental prowess: "Of mine own self," He said, "I can do nothing." "The Father within, He doeth the works."

As St. Paul said, God "is able to do exceeding abundantly above all that we ask or think, according to the Power that worketh in us."

There is within every man a tremendous latent power which is capable not only of solving every problem, healing every disease, dissolving every difficulty and adjusting every negative state of mind, but abundantly able, if he will use it, to keep him in a perennial state of wholeness and success. It is the duty of religion therefore to teach man how to employ and apply this Power, not only to all his hurts but to insulate him from them.

The Law says that whatever you consciously affirm and inwardly accept the Power will create for you. Thus to change your destiny and to get what you want, "your intellect, your will and your feeling must agree with your affirmations." It is not enough to make a lot of abstract statements such as "God is my help in every need;" "God is a very present help in trouble;" "God is Good;" "God is Love;" "God is All;" and then leave them dangling in the air. They must be integrated with the Law of Life. If the affirmations are to be effective and if they are to accomplish the things they are sent out to do, then we must not only hold and think right thoughts but we must also loose them in the Law. They must be inwardly accepted and believed in.

SPECIALIZING THE POWER

"Physician, heal thyself" means that every man must adapt the Power to his own needs. He must specialize It through his own thought. Our next step then is to see how Life operates through us and how It becomes the things we want. The Power is faith in the Good, and the tools are right thoughts, words and ideas. Let us go forth then and learn how to use them.

Second, we shall take the perfect image representing the opposite, or positive condition of the above negative, and turn our attention to it. If the negative condition were sickness, we would turn our attention upon an affirmation of health. If it were discord, we would turn our attention upon harmony. If it were poverty, we would turn out attention to opulence, and so forth.

We will not seek to destroy the negative condition by will power or force but, as Jesus suggested, by turning away from it—by lifting our thoughts to God and by holding in mind the right attitude or perfect image.

The result will be a complete transfer of power from the negative condition to the positive condition. Consciousness will become so engrossed in building the perfect image that the imperfect image will have nothing more to live upon. It will die from lack of attention, because attention was the only power it had.

And this, my friend, is the whole meaning of changing your thought. When consciousness has been transferred from an undesirable condition to a desirable one, the undesirable condition dies. It dies because it has nothing more to feed upon and will in time completely disappear. And as more and more attention is given to the perfect image, more and more firmly will it be established in your self.

When St. Paul said, "Be not overcome of evil, but overcome evil with Good," it was meant that we were to eliminate the negative by accentuating the positive. It is not a matter of fighting the wrong, but of creating the right. The condition is changed not because we change the nature of the power but because we alter our position toward it. This is a very simple method and can be used by anybody in removing negative conditions from mind and body. If the requirements are fulfilled the method will work perfectly and successfully in every instance. All things work together for good to those who keep their minds off self and on God. By dwelling on the Good, we cause all things to work for our good.

The larger interpretation of religion does not rest upon the question of man's churchmanship —whether he is good or bad, religious or irreligious. It rests upon the questions, whether his idea of God is rational—does he have a travelled path to His Presence; and whether he has the consciousness of His Presence. Does he see Him constantly as the Universal Source, bestowing only that which is Good and manifesting according to thought and belief, or as a fickle and unpredictable Being, interacting between reflexes of good and evil, rewards and punishments?

GOD IS NOT AN ALMSHOUSE KEEPER

God is not an almshouse keeper nor an Aladdin's lamp, whose chief business it is to fill the vacant and waste places in our lives and to gratify our desires. God is a Presence to be felt and a Friend to be cultivated. He will give us what we need when we love Him with all the heart, all the mind, all the strength and all the soul. And without love and daily communion we cannot hope to receive the greater gifts which such a love bestows. "I am God and beside me there is none else."

The Power that shapes our lives is within ourselves. It is a Universal Wholeness which enters into us in such degree as we enter into It. It manifests through our thoughts, convictions and assertions. As we identify ourselves with It, It becomes us and enables us to do things which otherwise would be impossible. As we fail to identify ourselves with It, It lets us alone.

Jesus said: "Ye seek me, not because ye saw the miracles, but because ye did eat of the loaves, and were filled." If we think of Heaven as a sort of bag out of which to squeeze rabbits, dollars and silk flags. If our religious life is built merely around the petition, "Give us this day our daily bread," and if our chief interest centers in what we can get from God. Indeed, if the hope of receiving some blessing is the only thing that makes us bend the knee, then our fellowship with God will be broken. Our heaven will be wrecked because we have regarded it as a bargain counter. We will be in the same position toward God as the boy toward his family when he writes home only when he wants money.

Real prayer is not a petition to an unwilling God but a fellowship with God. It is not a magic wand but an attitude toward life. It is not an acquisition but an experience. It is not an attempt to hold God's attention but to let Him hold ours. It is a surrender of our will to His Will, a lifting of our life to His Life. Heaven does not promise a pot of money hanging on the end of a rainbow but a life that is free from want. It guarantees peace of mind and strength equal to any need.

BREAKING THE POWER OF CIRCUMSTANCE

"The most powerful astronomical observatories are built on the mountain tops, so the great lenses which sweep the heavens may not be obscured by dust, dirt, mists or fog floating in the atmosphere of the lowlands. To shut out the din, the constant noises which distract the mind; to be free from the thousand and one disturbing influences in our strenuous daily life, the things which warp and twist and distort us, it is necessary to rise to the Higher realms of thought and feeling, where we can breathe a purer, more invigorating air, get a clearer touch with the Divine."

The highest form of prayer is the prayer of uplifted thought, as when Jesus lifted His eyes to Heaven and said, "Father, I thank Thee that Thou hearest me. And I know that Thou hearest me always;" and when the Psalmist said, "I will lift up mine eyes unto the hills, from whence cometh my help." Before the elevator can go up the weights must come down. Before man can rise self must be left behind. St. Paul said: "Reckon ye also yourselves to be dead indeed unto sin, and alive unto God." That is, leave self out of your reckoning altogether. Be dead to self and alive to God. "It is no longer I that live, but Christ liveth in me."

When you realize that the painful and negative experiences of life can have power over you only so long as the personal sense of self is alive, only so long as you do your thinking and living on the lower plane away from the Father's House, then you shall break the power of environment of circumstances by raising your thoughts to God.

And what will be the result of such actions? We have the answer in the words of Christian D. Larson: "Every step that is taken in the raising of consciousness means more life, greater intelligence, greater freedom, greater demonstration, greater realization, more brilliant thinking and higher knowing. And when we go far enough in raising the consciousness, we shall enter the home of the soul; we shall enter the unending silence of Spirit; we shall enter the 'peace that passeth understanding;' we shall enter cosmic consciousness; we shall enter the realm of spiritual reality, where all things are perfect; we shall enter the Cosmos of the Limitless, where all power is given; we shall enter Life Itself—the Life Everlasting—

where immortality is discovered; we shall enter the light of Divine Intelligence—the brilliance of pure wisdom—where all things are known.

"Thus we understand the full and high meaning of this remarkable statement: 'Be still and know:' The farther we go into spiritual stillness, the more we shall know; and when we go far enough, we shall enter the light wherein anything may be known—even to know that 'I am God;' and this can only mean that we may, in that Secret place, meet the Most High 'face to face,' that we may actually look in upon that marvelous realm 'where the Infinite abides in smiling repose.' "

"I pray not," said Jesus in His great protection prayer, "that Thou shouldest take them out of this world, but that Thou shouldest keep them from the evil. They are not of the world, even as I am not of the world. Sanctify them through Thy Truth: Thy word is Truth." When we have developed the consciousness of God to such an extent that it becomes a part of us, and our every thought radiates it, then we have reached a place in mind where trouble cannot affect us and nothing can do us harm. We shall no longer be torn asunder by outside forces, but shall rest confidently and triumphantly on the strength of an Interior Power. We shall meet our problem thenceforth not through our own minds, but through God's Mind.

• •

ACKNOWLEDGMENT

The Author wishes to make grateful acknowledgment to—

Unity Publications

Christian D. Larson

Henry Thomas Hamblin

Ernest Holmes

Emmet Fox

Orison Swett Marden

Joseph R. Sizoo, D.D.

The Rev. E. Stanley Jones

Bishop Austin Pardue

for quotations and suggestions used in the preparation of this book.

www.ingramcontent.com/pod-product-compliance
Ingram Content Group UK Ltd.
Pitfield, Milton Keynes, MK11 3LW, UK
UKHW040855120125
453454UK00001B/95